A Taste of

by Karen Billideau

Edited by Kathleen Bryant

Northland Publishing

To Brian,
your love and support have made
so many things possible.

Compilation © 2005 by Northland Publishing
Cover photo © Ross Durant/PictureArts
Back Cover: Courtesy of Arizona Historical Society Museum at Papago Park
Photography © 2005 by: Courtesy of Lake County (IL) Discovery Museum,
Curt Teich Postcard Archives, vintage postcards: front cover, IV, 14, 24, 36, 60, 68, 76, 84

www.northlandbooks.com

Composed in the United States of America
Printed in China

FIRST IMPRESSION 2006
ISBN-10: 0-87358-887-8 (sc)
ISBN-13: 978-0-87358-887-4 (sc)

06   07   08   09   10   5   4   3   2   1

Library of Congress Cataloging-in-Publication Data

Billideau, Karen.
A taste of Arizona / recipes by Karen Billideau ; text and compilation by Kathleen Bryant.
p. cm.
1. Cookery, American. 2. Cookery—Arizona. I. Bryant, Kathleen. II. Title.

TX715.B49774 2006

641.56791—dc22   2005049854

Publisher's Note: The recipes contained in this book are to be followed
exactly as written. Neither the publisher nor the author is responsible for
your specific health or allergy needs that may require medical supervision,
or for any adverse reactions to the recipes contained in this book.

CONTENTS

APPETIZERS

BROKEN ARROW BEAN DIP

Westerns introduced moviegoers to Arizona, from the street scenes of Old Tucson to the dramatic buttes of Monument Valley. The 1953 movie Broken Arrow starred Jimmy Stewart. Though the story takes place in southeastern Arizona, outdoor scenes were shot in Sedona's red rocks. Today, Broken Arrow Trail winds below the cliffs and buttes used as backdrop in the film.

Heat the vegetable oil in a medium saucepan. Sauté the onion and garlic. Add the beans and chiles and stir over low heat until bubbling. Serve with tortilla chips. *Makes about 2 cups*

2 tablespoons vegetable oil
1 onion, finely chopped
3 cloves garlic, minced
1 (15-ounce) can refried beans
1 (4-ounce) can diced green chiles

MEXICAN LAYERED DIP

Spread the bean dip in a 13 x 9-inch baking dish. Blend sour cream, salad dressing, and taco seasoning. Spread the sour cream mixture on top of the bean dip. Mash the avocados with lemon juice, salt, and pepper. Spread the avocado mixture over the sour cream layer. Arrange lettuce on top and sprinkle with tomatoes, green onions, and black olives. Cover with shredded cheese. Chill well and serve with tortilla chips. *Makes 10 to 12 servings*

2 (9-ounce) cans bean dip
8 ounces sour cream
1/2 cup salad dressing, Catalina or Italian
1 package taco seasoning
3 ripe avocados
Juice of 1/2 lemon
1/8 teaspoon salt
1/8 teaspoon pepper
2 cups shredded lettuce
3 tomatoes, chopped
1 cup green onions, chopped
1/4 cup black olives, chopped
1 cup shredded Monterey Jack and Colby cheeses

CATTLE RUSTLER'S DIP

Preheat oven to 350 degrees F. Combine cream cheese, milk, beef, and garlic powder in a bowl. Pour this mixture into a 9-inch pie pan. In another bowl, combine pecans and margarine and pour over the top of the beef mixture. Bake 20 minutes. Serve with tortilla chips. *Makes about 1 1/2 cups*

1 (8-ounce) package cream cheese, softened
2 tablespoons milk
5 ounces dried beef, chopped
1 teaspoon garlic powder
1/2 cup pecans, chopped
2 tablespoons melted margarine

RIMROCK REFRIED BEAN DIP

Preheat oven to 350 degrees F. Combine refried beans, olives, onions, taco sauce, and garlic salt with 1 1/2 cups of the shredded cheese. Spoon mixture into a 1-quart baking dish and sprinkle with the remaining 1/2 cup of cheese. Bake 30 minutes. Serve with tortilla chips. *Makes 3 cups*

1 (29-ounce) can refried beans
1 (4-ounce) can chopped black olives, drained
1 cup onions, chopped
1/2 cup taco sauce
1 teaspoon garlic salt
2 cups shredded Cheddar cheese

BRANDING IRON BEAN DIP

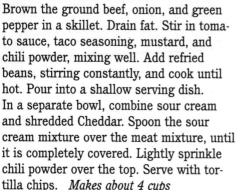

Brown the ground beef, onion, and green pepper in a skillet. Drain fat. Stir in tomato sauce, taco seasoning, mustard, and chili powder, mixing well. Add refried beans, stirring constantly, and cook until hot. Pour into a shallow serving dish. In a separate bowl, combine sour cream and shredded Cheddar. Spoon the sour cream mixture over the meat mixture, until it is completely covered. Lightly sprinkle chili powder over the top. Serve with tortilla chips. *Makes about 4 cups*

1 pound ground beef
1/2 cup onion, chopped
1/2 cup green bell pepper, chopped
1 (8-ounce) can tomato sauce
1 package taco seasoning mix
1 teaspoon powdered mustard
1 tablespoon chili powder
1 (15-ounce) can refried beans
1 (8-ounce) carton sour cream
1 cup shredded Cheddar cheese
Additional chili powder

ROBBER'S ROOST CHILES RELLENOS DIP

Preheat oven to 350 degrees F. Layer chiles and cheeses in a small, ungreased baking dish. Combine eggs and sour cream and pour over the top. Bake approximately 30 minutes, until the mixture is lightly browned on top and looks like a custard. Allow to stand 5 minutes before serving. *Makes 10 to 12 servings*

1 (4-ounce) can diced green chiles
2 cups shredded Monterey Jack cheese
2 cups shredded Cheddar cheese
2 eggs, beaten
1/2 cup sour cream

GUADALUPE GUACAMOLE

This village tucked within the greater Phoenix area was settled by Yaqui Indians who fled Mexico a century ago to avoid being deported for their religious practices. During Easter season, in the plaza between Our Lady of Guadalupe church and the Yaqui temple, tribal members perform centuries-old ceremonies that blend the Catholicism of Spanish missionaries with the deer dance.

In a medium bowl, mash the avocados with the lemon or lime juice. Add garlic, onion, tomato, salt, black pepper, cayenne, and chili powder. Refrigerate an hour for the flavors to blend. Serve with tortilla chips.
Makes about 3 cups

3 ripe avocados
3 tablespoons lime or lemon juice
3 cloves garlic, minced
1/2 onion, finely chopped
1 tomato, finely chopped
1 teaspoon salt
1/2 teaspoon ground black pepper
1/4 teaspoon cayenne
2 teaspoons chili powder

GRAND CANYON GUACAMOLE

Mash the avocados in a large bowl. Add garlic, onion, salt, pepper, olive oil, lime juice, tomato, cumin, and jalapeños. Blend together until almost smooth.
Makes 2 cups

2 large ripe avocados
5 cloves garlic, minced
1 onion, minced
1/2 teaspoon salt
1/4 teaspoon pepper
1 tablespoon olive oil
1 tablespoon lime juice
1 tomato, chopped
1/2 teaspoon ground cumin
1 (4-ounce) can chopped jalapeños

INDIAN GARDENS VEGETABLE DIP

Combine the cream cheese, mayonnaise, and sour cream in a bowl and beat at medium speed with an electric mixer. Add green pepper, onion, bacon, chiles, and olives. Add lemon juice to taste. Refrigerate at least 2 hours. Serve with an assortment of raw vegetables.
Makes 6 cups

2 (8-ounce) packages cream cheese, softened
1 cup mayonnaise
8 ounces sour cream
1 cup green bell pepper, finely chopped
1 cup red onion, finely chopped
1/4 cup bacon bits
1 (4-ounce) can green chiles
1 (4-ounce) can chopped ripe olives, drained
Lemon juice

CHUSKA CHILE-CHEESE DIP

Heat the oil in a medium skillet and sauté the onion and garlic. Add the green chiles, jalapeños, and tomatoes, breaking up the tomatoes with a spoon. Reduce heat and add cheeses. Cook until melted. Stir in the sour cream and cook just until heated through. Do not overcook. Serve with tortilla chips. *Makes about 4 cups*

1/4 cup vegetable oil
1 cup onion, chopped
6 cloves garlic, minced
1 (4-ounce) can diced green chiles
2 jalapeños, roasted, peeled, and chopped
1 (8-ounce) can stewed tomatoes
2 cups shredded Monterey Jack cheese
2 cups shredded sharp Cheddar cheese
8 ounces sour cream

KARTCHNER CAVERN GUACAMOLE CHIPS

The fabulous limestone formations in this "living" underground cavern south of Benson are tens of thousands of years old and still forming. Some sound like they came straight from the pages of a cookbook: turnip shields, bacon, soda straws, and moon milk.

Preheat broiler. Mash the avocados in a medium bowl. Stir in lemon juice, onion, mayonnaise, mustard, salt, and Tabasco. Set aside the guacamole mixture. Arrange chips evenly on a cookie sheet and sprinkle with shredded cheese. Drizzle with salsa and place under broiler just long enough to melt the cheese. Break chips apart and place on a serving plate. Top each chip with guacamole and sour cream. Serve immediately. *Makes 8 to 12 servings*

2 large ripe avocados
3 tablespoons lemon juice
1/4 cup onion, grated
1 tablespoon mayonnaise
2 tablespoons prepared mustard
1/2 teaspoon salt
1/4 teaspoon Tabasco
1 bag tortilla chips
2 cups shredded Monterey Jack cheese
1 (12-ounce) jar green chile salsa
1 cup sour cream

NORTH RIM NACHOS

This less-visited side of Grand Canyon National Park is hours from the bustle of the South Rim. Often inaccessible during winter snows, the North Rim is a cool and quiet getaway during summer months. These nachos would make a fine treat any time of year.

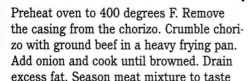

Preheat oven to 400 degrees F. Remove the casing from the chorizo. Crumble chorizo with ground beef in a heavy frying pan. Add onion and cook until browned. Drain excess fat. Season meat mixture to taste with salt and Tabasco.

Spread the beans in a 15 x 10-inch baking dish and cover with meat mixture. Sprinkle with green chiles, then top with cheese and drizzle with taco sauce. Bake uncovered 20 to 25 minutes, until heated through. Sprinkle with green onions and olives. Mound the mashed avocado in the center and top with sour cream. Serve with tortilla chips. *Makes about 12 servings*

1/2 pound chorizo sausage
1/2 pound ground beef
1 large onion, chopped
Salt
Tabasco
2 (15-ounce) cans refried beans
1 (4-ounce) can diced green chiles
2 cups shredded Monterey Jack cheese
3/4 cup taco sauce
1/2 cup green onions, chopped
1 (6-ounce) can sliced ripe olives
1 ripe avocado, mashed
8 ounces sour cream

SONOITA STUFFED BRIE

Wine country in the desert? A growing number of vintners are choosing Arizona's high, dry climate for their grapes. Visitors to Sonoita, a quiet town near the Arizona-Mexico border, can tour a half-dozen regional wineries offering Merlot, Petite Sirah, Sangiovese, Cabernet Sauvignon, and other varietals. Enjoy a glass with this elegant appetizer.

Combine the cream cheese, blue cheese, and sherry, stirring until the mixture is soft and easy to spread. Stir in the almonds and grapes. Slice the Brie in half through the middle, making two rounds. Spread the cream cheese mixture on the bottom round, place the other round on top, and cut into wedges. Serve with an assortment of crackers on the side.
Makes 6 to 8 servings

1 (3-ounce) package cream cheese, softened
1/4 cup crumbled blue cheese
2 tablespoons dry sherry
1/4 cup almonds, sliced
1/4 cup seedless grapes, sliced
1 round Brie cheese

SAGUARO CHILE-CHEESE SPREAD

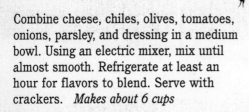

Combine cheese, chiles, olives, tomatoes, onions, parsley, and dressing in a medium bowl. Using an electric mixer, mix until almost smooth. Refrigerate at least an hour for flavors to blend. Serve with crackers. *Makes about 6 cups*

2 pounds shredded Monterey Jack cheese
1 (4-ounce) can diced green chiles
1 (4-ounce) can chopped olives, drained
4 tomatoes, chopped
1 bunch green onions, chopped
1/4 cup parsley, chopped
1 (8-ounce) bottle Italian salad dressing

CHINLE CHILE PINWHEELS

The town of Chinle (Navajo for "a place where water emerges from a canyon's mouth") is the gateway to Canyon de Chelly, where history and scenery combine to create one of Arizona's most stunning national monuments. During the 1920s, Cozy McSparron expanded the local trading post into a lodge, began offering canyon tours, and encouraged local weavers to develop the Chinle rug style, a striped design using vegetal dyes.

Combine cream cheese, sour cream, garlic, chiles, olives, chives, lime juice, and picante sauce until well blended. Spread a portion of this mixture on each of the tortillas. Roll up the tortillas and refrigerate them several hours, until firm. To serve, slice the tortillas into bite-sized pinwheels.
Makes about 8 to 10 servings

1 (8-ounce) package cream cheese, softened
1 (8-ounce) carton sour cream
3 cloves garlic, minced
1 (4-ounce) can diced green chiles
1 (4-ounce) can chopped ripe olives, drained
1/3 cup chives, chopped
Juice of one lime
1/3 cup picante sauce
6 flour tortillas

FLAGSTAFF FIRE WINGS

Gaze up at the San Francisco Peaks, snowcapped much of the year, and try to picture one massive volcano that blew its top a million years ago, creating a quartet of peaks: Humphrey, Agassiz, Doyle, and Fremont. Flagstaff is surrounded by cinder cones, lava domes, and other volcanic features. You can discover more about Flagstaff's fiery past at nearby Sunset Crater National Monument. Pair these wings with a bottle of brew from one of Flag's numerous microbreweries.

Rinse the chicken wings and pat dry. Combine the herbs, spices, and salt and set aside. Preheat the oil in a deep fryer. Deep-fry the wings in batches until golden brown. Drain on paper towels. Arrange the wings in a single layer in a baking dish and sprinkle them with the seasoning mixture. Keep warm until all the wings are cooked and seasoned. Serve with a ranch-style dressing and celery sticks.
Makes about 8 to 12 servings

3 pounds chicken wings
1 tablespoon cayenne
1 tablespoon ground black pepper
1 tablespoon white pepper
1 tablespoon garlic powder
1 tablespoon onion powder
1 tablespoon dried basil
1 tablespoon dried oregano
1 tablespoon salt
Vegetable oil for deep-frying

PARADISE VALLEY VEGGIE NUGGETS

More than a century ago, planners envisioned Paradise Valley as an agricultural paradise, with a 140-mile long ditch carrying water from the Salt River to farms and ranches. The Salt River Valley's first canal builders, the Hohokam, built canals a millennium ago to water their gardens of corn, beans, and squash. Stroll through your garden to find tasty additions to the zucchini and mushrooms called for in this recipe.

Slice the zucchini and mushrooms and chill them in the refrigerator. Preheat the oil in a deep fryer. Combine the eggs, salt, pepper, cayenne, garlic powder, beer, and vegetable oil in a medium bowl, mixing after each addition. Dip the vegetables in batter and deep-fry them until golden brown, one piece at a time to prevent them from sticking together. Drain on paper towels. Serve with a ranch-style dressing for dipping.
Makes about 4 to 6 servings

1 large zucchini, sliced
10 mushrooms, sliced
Vegetable oil for deep-frying
2 eggs, beaten
1 teaspoon salt
1/2 teaspoon black pepper
1/2 teaspoon cayenne pepper
1/4 teaspoon garlic powder
1/2 cup beer
1 cup all-purpose flour
3 tablespoons vegetable oil

PICACHO PEPPER PECANS

The jagged silhouette of Picacho Peak is a beacon to travelers on I-10 between Tucson and Eloy. Groves of pecan trees, slender and graceful, grow along the freeway near the rocky basalt peak. In spring, orange poppies, red paintbrush, and other wildflowers spice up the trails at Picacho Peak State Park. This spicy treat would make a gourmet pack snack or an irresistible appetizer.

Preheat oven to 325 degrees F. Melt the butter in a large skillet and add Worcestershire sauce, salt, cinnamon, cloves, garlic powder, cayenne, Tabasco, and pecans. Stir until all the pecans are well coated. Place them in a single layer on a cookie sheet and bake 30 minutes. *Makes 4 cups*

4 tablespoons butter
2 tablespoons Worcestershire sauce
1 teaspoon salt
1 teaspoon cinnamon
1/8 teaspoon ground cloves
1/2 teaspoon garlic powder
1/4 teaspoon cayenne pepper
1/3 teaspoon (about 20 drops) Tabasco
4 cups pecan halves

TEMPE SUN DEVIL SHRIMP

Home to Arizona State University, Tempe is youth-oriented and hip, especially on game weekends, when Mill Avenue turns into a people watcher's paradise from the shores of Town Lake all the way to Sun Devil Stadium, where the NFL's Arizona Cardinals also hang their helmets. Serve these spicy shrimp at the pre-game party, and you'll make points with your guests.

Combine white wine, vinegar, ketchup, mustard, horseradish, paprika, cayenne, garlic powder, salt, and oil in a large mixing bowl and mix until well blended. Add shrimp and marinate in the refrigerator at least 3 hours. Drain shrimp and serve with pepper slices. *Makes about 6 servings*

1/2 cup dry white wine
1/2 cup wine vinegar
2 tablespoons ketchup
2 tablespoons mustard
1 teaspoon prepared horseradish
1/2 teaspoon paprika
1/2 teaspoon cayenne
1/4 teaspoon garlic powder
1/2 teaspoon salt
1 cup vegetable oil
1 pound cooked shrimp
1 red or yellow bell pepper, sliced

SANTA RITA SPINACH TOMATOES

Preheat oven to 350 degrees F. Cook spinach in a large saucepan, adding bouillon cubes and following package directions. Drain, cool, and press out excess liquid. Salt the tomato halves and drain them on paper towels, cut side down, to remove some of the moisture.

Combine the spinach, bread crumbs, butter, onion, garlic, pepper, cayenne, egg, and half the Parmesan cheese. Mix well. Arrange the tomatoes in a shallow baking dish, cut side up. Fill each with spinach mixture. Sprinkle with the remaining Parmesan and bake 15 minutes, until heated through. *Serves 6*

1 (10-ounce) package frozen chopped spinach
2 chicken bouillon cubes
Salt
3 large tomatoes, halved
1 cup soft bread crumbs
1/2 cup butter, melted
1/2 cup onion, chopped
1 clove garlic, minced
1/2 teaspoon ground black pepper
1/4 teaspoon cayenne
1 egg, beaten
1/2 cup grated Parmesan cheese

MULE MOUNTAIN EMPANADAS

Preheat oven to 450 degrees F. Combine beef and onion in a skillet. Cook over medium heat, until meat is browned. Drain excess fat. Stir in cheese, ketchup, chili powder, and Tabasco, cooking until cheese is melted.

Roll out the pastry and cut the dough in circles with a 2 1/2-inch cookie cutter. Spoon 1 heaping teaspoon of filling in the center of each circle. Fold in half and seal the edges. Bake 10 to 15 minutes, or until lightly browned, turning once.
Makes 48

1/2 pound ground beef
1/2 cup onion, chopped
1 cup shredded Cheddar cheese
1/4 cup ketchup
2 teaspoons chili powder
1/4 teaspoon Tabasco
2 (11-ounce) packages piecrust pastry

PRESIDIO POTATO OMELET

A town within a city, Tucson's Presidio is the original walled settlement of the Presidio of San Agustín, dating to 1775. La Casa Cordova and other historic buildings preserve glimpses of early Arizona, when Spanish colonists (and later, wealthy Americans) were protected from raiding Apaches by the Presidio's twelve-foot adobe walls. Try this potato omelet for terrific tapas, or Spanish-style appetizers.

Heat the oil in a large nonstick skillet. Add potatoes, one slice at a time, in layers. After each layer of potatoes, add a layer of onion. Cook over low heat, turning often. Do not allow the potatoes to brown. Place the cooked potatoes and onion in a colander to drain, reserving 3 tablespoons of the oil.

Preheat oven to 325 degrees F. In a large bowl, beat the eggs until foamy. Add parsley, pimientos, and potatoes, seasoning with salt and pepper. Make sure potatoes are covered by the egg mixture. Set mixture aside to soak for 15 minutes.

Heat the reserved oil in a nonstick, oven-proof skillet. When the oil begins to smoke, add the potato-egg mixture, spreading it evenly over the bottom of the pan. Lower heat and cook 4 minutes. Transfer the skillet to the oven and bake 20 minutes, or until the omelet is golden brown on top and firm to the touch. Place on a serving platter and cool to room temperature. Cut into slices and serve.

Makes about 8 servings

1 cup olive oil
4 large potatoes, peeled and very thinly sliced
1 large onion, thinly sliced
4 eggs
1 tablespoon parsley, chopped
2 tablespoons pimientos, chopped
Salt and pepper

SALADS

SUPERSTITION SPINACH-POPPY SEED SALAD

Mix sugar, salt, mustard, onion powder, vinegar, and lime juice. Stir until sugar dissolves. Slowly whisk in oil. Add poppy seeds and chill. Pour over mixed greens before serving. *Makes 8 to 10 servings*

1/2 cup sugar
1 teaspoon salt
1 teaspoon dry mustard
1/2 teaspoon onion powder
1/2 cup white balsamic vinegar
1 tablespoon lime juice
1 cup salad oil
1 1/2 tablespoons poppy seeds
2 bunches of spinach, washed and trimmed
2 bunches of watercress, washed

SCOTTSDALE DILLY POTATO SALAD

Every April, Scottsdale celebrates its status as a cuisine capital with the Culinary Festival, offering a tasty menu of events that includes the Great Arizona Picnic, when local restaurants bring their best to the lush green lawn of Civic Center Plaza. Take this potato salad to your next picnic.

Dice the cooked potatoes and place in a large bowl with chopped eggs. Mix mayonnaise, pickles, mustard, and onions, seasoning to taste with salt, pepper, and celery salt. Stir dressing into potatoes and eggs. Chill. *Makes 4 to 6 servings*

6 large red potatoes, cooked in their peels
2 medium hard-boiled eggs, peeled and chopped
1/4 cup dill pickle, chopped
1 cup mayonnaise
1 teaspoon dry mustard
4 green onions, chopped
Salt and pepper
Celery salt

GOLDMINE FIVE BEAN SALAD

Place beans, bell pepper, and onions in a large bowl. Combine vegetable oil, vinegar, sugar, garlic powder, and salt in a jar and shake until well blended. Add pepper to taste. Pour the dressing over the beans and vegetables and toss to coat thoroughly. Cover and refrigerate overnight to marinate. Toss again before serving.
Makes 10 to 12 servings

1 (15-ounce) can pinto beans, drained
1 (15-ounce) can black beans, drained
1 (15-ounce) can garbanzo beans, drained
1 (15-ounce) can cut green beans, drained
1 (15-ounce) can cut wax beans, drained
2 green bell peppers, chopped
2 bunches green onions, chopped
2/3 cup vegetable oil
2/3 cup vinegar
2/3 cup sugar
1/4 teaspoon garlic powder
1 teaspoon salt
Pepper

COLORADO RIVER CAULIFLOWER SALAD

Whisk together the oil, ketchup, sugar, lemon juice, salt and paprika in a large bowl. Add olives, cauliflower, bell pepper, and onion. Stir well to coat the vegetables. Marinate for several hours or overnight before serving. *Makes 4 servings*

1/4 cup olive oil
1/2 cup ketchup
1/4 cup sugar
1 tablespoon lemon juice
1 teaspoon salt
1 teaspoon paprika
1 cup green olives, chopped
4 cups cauliflower florets
1/2 cup green bell pepper, chopped
1/2 cup red onion, chopped

OAK CREEK ORANGE AND SPINACH SALAD

Combine oil, sugar, vinegar, and ketchup in a jar and shake to blend. Remove stems from spinach leaves. Place the spinach in a large bowl and add mandarin oranges, mushrooms, onion, and pecans. Toss to mix. Add the dressing just before serving. *Makes 4 servings*

1/2 cup salad oil
1/4 cup granulated sugar
1/4 cup vinegar
1/4 cup ketchup
1 bunch spinach, washed and drained
1 (11-ounce) can mandarin oranges, drained
1 cup mushrooms, sliced
1 red onion, sliced into rings
1/2 cup pecans, toasted

SABINO CANYON BLACK BEAN SALAD

Mix chili powder, cumin, cayenne, garlic powder, and wild rice in a large bowl. Add beans, lettuce, onions, cucumber, tomatoes, avocado, cheeses, and corn chips, mixing together. Just before serving, add salad dressing and stir to combine.
Makes 8 to 10 servings

1 teaspoon chili powder
1 teaspoon ground cumin
1 teaspoon cayenne
1 teaspoon garlic powder
1 cup cooked wild rice
1 1/2 cups cooked black beans
1 head romaine lettuce
1 head leaf lettuce
1 bunch green onions, chopped
1 cucumber, sliced
2 tomatoes, chopped
2 avocados, chopped
1 cup shredded pepper Jack cheese
1 cup shredded Cheddar cheese
2 cups blue corn chips
French salad dressing

SPANISH CHICKEN SALAD

Combine the oil and vinegar, seasoning to taste with salt and pepper. Place the chicken, shredded lettuce, and onion in a bowl. Toss gently with dressing. Divide mixture and spoon it onto lettuce leaves. Slice the avocados. Arrange the avocado, orange, and radish slices around the chicken mixture.
Makes 6 servings

1/2 cup olive oil
1/4 cup red wine vinegar
Salt and pepper
3 1/2 cups cooked chicken strips
1 head lettuce, shredded
1 red onion, thinly sliced
Lettuce leaves
2 avocados
2 oranges, peeled and sliced
1 bunch radishes, sliced

PIÑON CHICKEN SALAD

A few miles north of the Hopi villages on sprawling Black Mesa, the Navajo town of Piñon is surrounded, like much of northern Arizona, by piñon-juniper woodland. For centuries, piñon trees have provided fuel, food, and pitch, used by the Navajo to seal baskets and pottery. Pound for pound, piñon nuts, gathered in late August, boast as much protein as steak.

Preheat the oven to 350 degrees F. Toast the pine nuts in the oven for 5 minutes. Steam spinach and chop it coarsely. Combine pine nuts and spinach with the 2 tablespoons melted butter, onions, ricotta, egg yolk, salt, and pepper.

Increase oven temperature to 375 degrees F. Place prosciutto on chicken. Spread with spinach filling and roll up from small end. Place chicken rolls seam side down in a nonstick casserole dish. Mix 3 tablespoons melted butter with lemon juice. Spoon over chicken. Bake 20 to 25 minutes, basting with pan juices, until chicken and filling are cooked through. Chill.

Slice chilled chicken rolls and arrange on lettuce leaves. Mix additional lemon juice with mayonnaise to garnish each serving. *Makes 4 to 6 servings*

1/4 cup pine nuts
1 pound spinach, washed and trimmed
2 tablespoons butter, melted
6 green onions, chopped
1/2 cup ricotta cheese
1 egg yolk
1/2 teaspoon seasoned salt
1/4 teaspoon pepper
2 slices prosciutto
2 boneless chicken breasts, pounded
   to 1/4 inch thin
3 tablespoons butter, melted
3 tablespoons lemon juice
Lettuce leaves
Additional lemon juice
4 tablespoons mayonnaise

COTTONWOOD CHICKEN SALAD

Arizona's rural roots still hold in Verde Valley towns like Cornville, Clarkdale, and Cottonwood. Orchards irrigated by the waters of the Verde River offer a bounty of produce, including apples, peaches, and pomegranates, the ingredient that makes this no ordinary chicken salad.

Combine all ingredients in a mixing bowl, stirring thoroughly. Serve with crackers or rolls. *Makes 2 to 4 servings*

1 (3.5-ounce) can chicken
1/2 cup raisins
1/2 cup sour cream
1/2 cup mayonnaise
3 slices canned pineapple, chopped
1/4 cup pomegranate jelly
Sliced fruit for garnish
Assorted crackers or rolls

CHINO VALLEY CHICKEN SALAD

Mix chicken, rice, grapes, celery, apples, and cashews in a large bowl. Add the mayonnaise and mix thoroughly. Dissolve the curry powder in hot water, blend with the soy sauce, and toss with the rest of the salad. Refrigerate until serving.
Makes 8 servings

4 chicken breasts, cooked and diced
2 cups cooked wild rice
1 cup red seedless grapes
1 cup celery, diced
1 cup apple, diced
1 cup cashews, slivered
2/3 cup mayonnaise
3 teaspoons curry powder
2 tablespoons hot water
1/4 cup soy sauce

COCHISE COUNTY TURKEY PISTACHIO SALAD

Southeastern Arizona's Cochise County is named for the great Apache leader Cochise. From 1860 to 1872, Cochise's band led the United States Army on a chase through the rocky mountain ranges of southeastern Arizona. Today, in the county's rich valleys, farmers raise chiles, pecans, pistachios, and other crops.

Combine turkey, grapes, green onion, and 1/2 cup of the pistachios in a medium mixing bowl. Coarsely chop the remaining 1/2 cup of pistachios and set aside. Stir together mayonnaise, sour cream, lemon juice, and dill or tarragon in a small mixing bowl. Fold dressing into turkey mixture. Season to taste with salt and pepper. Before serving, arrange on salad greens and sprinkle with chopped pistachios.
Makes 4 to 6 servings

3 cups shredded cooked turkey
1 cup seedless green grapes, halved
1 small green onion, chopped
1 cup shelled pistachios, divided in half
2 tablespoons mayonnaise
2 tablespoons sour cream
2 teaspoons lemon juice
3/4 teaspoon fresh dill or tarragon, minced
Salt and pepper
Salad greens

TUMBLEWEED SMOKED TURKEY AND APPLE SALAD

Whisk together the vinegar, olive oil, Dijon mustard, lemon pepper, and salt. Combine lettuce, carrot, tomatoes, turkey, apples, and walnuts in a large bowl. Toss with dressing.   *Makes 4 servings*

1/4 cup cider vinegar
1/2 cup olive oil
1 tablespoon Dijon mustard
1 teaspoon lemon pepper
1 teaspoon salt
1 head romaine lettuce, washed and torn
    into bite-size pieces
1 carrot, grated
10 cherry tomatoes, cut in half
8-ounces smoked turkey, sliced into strips
4 apples, sliced with peel on
1/2 cup walnuts, chopped

CONQUISTADOR BEEF SALAD

Combine salsa, oil, vinegar, and onion in a large bowl. Add roast beef, stirring to coat. Cover and refrigerate at least 1 hour. Arrange beef mixture on lettuce leaves and garnish with tomato, olives, and sliced avocado. *Makes 3 to 4 servings*

1 cup medium salsa
3 tablespoons vegetable oil
2 tablespoons red wine vinegar
1/2 cup red onion, chopped
1 pound beef roast, cooked and sliced
   into strips
Lettuce leaves
2 tomatoes, sliced
1/2 cup ripe olives
1 avocado

SUMMERHAVEN STEAK SALAD

Summerhaven, a village on the side of Mt. Lemmon, began as a cool summer retreat for Tucson residents, hence its name. Driving up the 9,157-foot mountain is comparable to driving all the way to Canada from the Sonoran Desert, due to biological life zones that change with elevation. The Santa Catalinas and other southern Arizona mountains are called sky islands because they are havens for towering pines, bears, and wildflowers, as well as campers and hikers.

Combine vinegar, olive oil, and Worcestershire sauce in a jar. Season to taste with salt and pepper and shake well to blend. Tear the lettuce into bite-size pieces and place in a large salad bowl. Shave the carrot with a vegetable peeler and add to the lettuce. Slice the avocados and add to salad bowl with steak and Parmesan cheese. Toss lightly with dressing just before serving. *Makes 4 servings*

1/4 cup wine vinegar
1/2 cup olive oil
1/4 cup Worcestershire sauce
Salt and pepper
1 head romaine lettuce
1/2 cup shredded Cheddar cheese
1 large carrot
3 avocados
1 medium red onion, sliced
1 pound steak, cooked and thinly sliced
1/4 cup grated Parmesan cheese

PHOENIX GRAPEFRUIT SALAD

On spring days in the Valley of the Sun (a nickname for the greater Phoenix area), breezes often carry the voluptuous scent of citrus blossoms. One of Arizona's five C's (the other four are climate, cotton, cattle, and copper), citrus was a cornerstone of the state's economy. Though many large orchards have made way for housing, orange, lemon, and grapefruit trees still scent the breezes, and locally grown fruit is sold at roadside stands and traded across backyard fences.

Combine oil, grapefruit zest, grapefruit and lemon juices, honey, paprika, and salt in a jar. Chill. Arrange grapefruit, oranges, strawberries, avocado, banana, and cantaloupe in a large salad bowl. Shake chilled dressing and pour over salad before serving.   *Makes 4 to 6 servings*

2/3 cup salad oil
1 teaspoon grapefruit zest
1/3 cup grapefruit juice
2 tablespoons lemon juice
2 tablespoons honey
1/2 teaspoon paprika
1/2 teaspoon salt
2 grapefruits, sectioned
2 oranges, sectioned
1 pint strawberries
2 medium avocados, sliced
1 banana, sliced
1/2 cantaloupe, diced

FORT MCDOWELL FRUIT SALAD

Many Arizona Indian communities offer gaming and entertainment at casinos located throughout the state. Twenty miles from Phoenix, the Fort McDowell Yavapai Nation hosts keno, cards, and slots. You'll hit the jackpot when you make this colorful fruit salad.

Place orange slices in a large bowl with pears and grapes. Combine orange juice, lemon juice, sugar, and cinnamon in a small bowl and combine thoroughly. Pour over fruit. Chill at least 2 hours. Sprinkle with pistachios just before serving.   *Makes 6 servings*

2 oranges, peeled and sliced crosswise
2 pears, peeled, sliced, and dipped in
    lemon juice
1 cup red seedless grapes
Juice of 1 orange
2 teaspoons lemon juice
1 tablespoon packed brown sugar
1/4 teaspoon cinnamon
1/2 cup chopped pistachios

GREETINGS FROM GRAND CANYON ARIZ.

SOUPS

AGUA FRIA AVOCADO SOUP

Puree avocados and chicken broth in a blender. Season to taste with salt and pepper. Slowly stir in cream. Chill. Add cognac and sherry just before serving.
Makes 4 servings

2 large avocados, diced
2 cups chicken broth
Salt and pepper
2 cups whipping cream
2 tablespoons cognac
2 tablespoons sherry

GADSONIA GAZPACHO

Gadsonia, one name tossed around for Arizona Territory, recognized James Gadsden, the United States Minister to Mexico. He negotiated the 1853 Gadsden Purchase, in which the United States bought 30 million acres from Mexico at about 33 cents an acre, adding Arizona's southern half.

Mix celery, bell pepper, onion, cucumber, tomatoes, tomato soup, water, juice, salad dressing, vinegar, salt, and pepper. Season to taste with garlic salt, Tabasco, and Worcestershire sauce. Refrigerate at least 4 hours to blend flavors.
Makes about 8 servings

1 cup celery, chopped
1 cup green bell pepper, chopped
1 cup onion, chopped
1/2 cup cucumber, chopped
1 cup tomatoes, chopped
1 (11-ounce) can condensed tomato soup
1 soup can water
1 (12-ounce) can vegetable juice
1 tablespoon Italian salad dressing
1 tablespoon wine vinegar
1/4 teaspoon salt
1/8 teaspoon pepper
Garlic salt
Tabasco
Worcestershire sauce

ARIZONA ZUCCHINI SOUP

Place the zucchini and a little water in a covered saucepan. Cook about 20 minutes, or until zucchini is crisp-tender. Drain. Puree the zucchini, milk, and stock in a blender. Melt the butter in a large saucepan and sauté onion until transparent. Add zucchini mixture, salt, and pepper. Cover and simmer over low heat 5 minutes.   *Makes 6 servings*

3 pounds zucchini, diced
4 cups milk
2 cups chicken stock
3 tablespoons butter
1/4 cup onion, chopped
1 1/2 teaspoons salt
1/2 teaspoon pepper

RUBY RED PEPPER SOUP

Like visiting ghost towns? Arizona has more than 250. During the late 1800s, the town of Ruby was a busy mining camp, as were many others within the Coronado National Forest. Today, most are in ruins, but for those adventurous enough to face rough back roads, "ghost towning" can be a poignant reminder of how time marches on.

Heat the oil and butter in a large skillet. Sauté the bell peppers, carrots, onion, and pear until tender. Add the broth and red pepper flakes, seasoning to taste with cayenne, salt, and black pepper. Bring to a boil. Reduce heat, cover, and simmer 30 minutes. Allow mixture to cool, then purée in a food processor. Reheat the soup before serving and garnish with tarragon.
Makes 6 servings

1 tablespoon olive oil
4 tablespoons butter
6 red bell peppers, thinly sliced
3 carrots, sliced
1 cup onion, chopped
1 pear, peeled and quartered
1 quart chicken broth
1 tablespoon red pepper flakes
Cayenne
Salt
Ground black pepper
Fresh tarragon

GREENLEE GREEN CHILE SOUP

Melt butter in large pot and add oil. Sauté garlic until lightly browned. Remove garlic and set aside. Sauté onion until tender. Add paprika and sauté for 1 minute. Add broth, tomatoes, chiles, and chili powder. Season with salt and pepper. Bring to a boil, reduce heat, and simmer 20 minutes. Slowly stir in yogurt and cook over low heat, just until heated through. Do not boil. Ladle into soup bowls and sprinkle with cheese and cilantro.
Makes 6 servings

2 tablespoons butter
1 tablespoon olive oil
5 cloves garlic, chopped
1 onion, chopped
1 tablespoon cilantro, chopped
2 teaspoons paprika
4 cups chicken broth
1 1/2 pounds tomatoes, chopped
1 (4-ounce) can diced green chiles
1/4 teaspoon chili powder
Salt and pepper
2 cups plain yogurt
1 cup shredded Cheddar cheese

VAQUERO BLACK BEAN SOUP

Sort and rinse the beans, cover with water, and soak overnight. Drain the beans and place them in a pot with water, salt pork, beef, carrot, onion, cloves, mace, and cayenne. Cover and simmer 3 hours. Pour soup into a large tureen. Add the sherry and garnish with lemon slices.
Makes 4 to 6 servings

2 cups dried black beans
12 cups water
1/4 pound salt pork
1/2 pound lean beef, cut into pieces
1 cup carrot, chopped
1 onion, chopped
3 whole cloves
1/2 teaspoon ground mace
Cayenne
1/2 cup sherry
1 lemon, sliced

KAYENTA KIDNEY BEAN SOUP

The Navajo Nation town of Kayenta is the gateway to Monument Valley Tribal Park, which sprawls across Arizona's northern edge into Utah. The Valley's buttes and spires play a dramatic role in dozens of movies and advertisements. Local guides offer jeep and horseback tours that wind between towering sandstone formations including the Mittens, Three Sisters, Totem Pole, and Yeibichai.

Heat the oil in a Dutch oven and cook the meat until it loses its pink color. Stir in the garlic and red pepper flakes. Add chili powder, cumin, oregano, salt, masa, and pepper, stirring to blend. Slowly add the broth and tomato sauce. Simmer 2 to 3 hours, stirring occasionally. Add the salsa and beans and simmer another 30 minutes. Garnish with cheese before serving.
Makes 4 to 6 servings

1/4 cup olive oil
3 pounds ground round
6 cloves garlic, minced
1 teaspoon red pepper flakes
5 tablespoons chili powder
1 teaspoon ground cumin
1 tablespoon dried oregano
2 teaspoons salt
3 tablespoons masa
1/2 teaspoon ground black pepper
1 (14-ounce) can beef broth
1 (8-ounce) can tomato sauce
1/4 cup salsa
2 (15-ounce) cans kidney beans
Sharp Cheddar cheese, shredded

POLACCA POSOLE

The Hopi village of Polacca sits below the cliffs of First Mesa. At the end of the nineteenth century, First Mesa potter Nampeyo recreated prehistoric designs and revitalized the tradition of Hopi pottery. Her descendants are among many potters who call Polacca home.

Place all ingredients in a large, heavy-bottomed pot or Dutch oven. Cover with water. Bring to a boil, then reduce heat to a simmer and continue cooking, covered, for about an hour. Uncover and cook another 1 1/2 to 2 hours, stirring occasionally and adding water as needed. Adjust seasonings before serving.

Makes 6 to 8 servings

1/2 pound hominy
1 onion, chopped
1 tablespoon red pepper flakes
1 pound oxtails, cut into pieces
3 cloves garlic, minced
2 tablespoons ground cumin
1 tablespoon dried oregano
1 (15-ounce) can diced tomatoes
1/2 teaspoon salt
1/2 teaspoon ground black pepper

TORTOLITA TORTILLA SOUP

Combine fish stock, tomato sauce, celery, onion, bell pepper, tomatoes, white pepper, garlic powder, oregano, and bay leaf in a pot. Season to taste with salt. Bring to a boil and simmer 20 to 30 minutes.

In the meantime, preheat oil. Cut the tortillas into strips and deep-fry until crisp. Drain on paper towels. Just before serving, divide tortilla strips between four bowls and sprinkle them with shredded cheeses. Ladle soup over tortillas and cheese.
Makes 4 servings

2 1/2 cups fish stock
1/4 cup tomato sauce
1/4 cup celery, diced
1/4 cup onion, diced
1/4 cup green bell pepper, diced
1/4 cup tomatoes, diced
1 teaspoon ground white pepper
1 teaspoon garlic powder
1 teaspoon dried oregano
1 bay leaf
Salt
Oil for deep-frying
4 corn tortillas
1 cup shredded Monterey Jack and Cheddar cheeses

AMBOS NOGALES MENUDO

A traditional post-fiesta remedy, menudo (tripe soup) is often a treasured family recipe. The town of Nogales straddles the border, and on both (ambos) sides you'll find a colorful blending of cultures.

Place beef and tripe in a large pot. Add garlic, onions, red pepper flakes, salt, oregano, chili powder, coriander, and water. Cover, bring to boil, reduce heat, and simmer 6 hours, or until tripe is very tender. Add hominy and simmer 30 minutes longer. Remove bones and adjust seasonings. Sprinkle with chopped cilantro before serving.   *Makes 8 to 10 servings*

4 pounds beef shins (instruct butcher to cut these into short lengths)
3 pounds tripe, cut into 1/2-inch pieces
5 cloves garlic, minced
2 cups onions, chopped
1 tablespoon red pepper flakes
2 teaspoons salt
2 teaspoons dried oregano
1 teaspoon ground coriander
4 quarts water
2 (15-ounce) cans hominy, drained
Cilantro, chopped

COWBELLE ALBÓNDIGAS

A group of women on isolated ranches in southeast Arizona started the Cowbelles in 1939 for support and fun. Swapping recipes and planning dances quickly expanded to such community-oriented activities as researching stock brand histories or fundraising for various charities, and the Cowbelles now have members in thirty states.

Soak bread cubes in milk until moistened. Mix with ground beef, chorizo, egg, and 1/2 teaspoon seasoned salt. Chill mixture 30 minutes. Meanwhile, combine celery, cilantro, onion, carrot, zucchini, broth, and tomatoes in a large pot. Bring to a boil, reduce heat, cover, and simmer 15 to 20 minutes. Shape meat mixture into balls. Add to soup, cover, and simmer 45 minutes, or until meat is done. Add additional seasoned salt and pepper to taste.
Makes 8 servings

1 cup bread cubes
1/4 cup milk
1/2 pound lean ground beef
1/2 pound chorizo sausage
1 egg
1/2 teaspoon seasoned salt
1 cup celery, sliced
1/2 cup fresh cilantro, chopped
1 cup carrots, sliced
2 cups zucchini, sliced
2 1/2 cups beef broth
1 (28-ounce) can tomatoes
Seasoned salt
Pepper

FIESTA BOWL

Throughout Arizona, the traditions of Mexico, Spain, and Native tribes blend with those of Anglo settlers, past and present. Starting New Year's Day with the Fiesta Bowl in Tempe and encompassing festivals, rodeos, pow-wows, and other get-togethers the rest of the year, Arizona's celebrations have a multicultural flair. This colorful soup blends the flavors of the Southwest: hominy, tortillas, and of course, chiles.

Melt butter in a heavy-bottomed pot and sauté onion for 5 minutes. Add rice and cook, stirring, until rice is opaque. Add broth, cumin, garbanzo beans, hominy, chiles, and chicken. Cook 20 minutes. Season to taste with salt and pepper. Garnish with chopped red bell pepper, if desired. Serve with grated cheese and warm tortillas. *Makes 8 servings*

4 tablespoons butter
1 large onion, chopped
1 1/3 cups raw white rice
3 quarts chicken broth
1 teaspoon ground cumin
2 (15-ounce) cans garbanzo beans, undrained
2 (15-ounce) cans golden hominy, undrained
2 (4-ounce) cans diced green chiles
2 cups cooked chicken, diced
Salt and pepper
Red bell pepper, chopped (optional)
Monterey Jack cheese, grated
Flour tortillas

CHIRACAHUA CHEESE SOUP

Heat the oil in a large saucepan and sauté onion, green onions, and garlic until tender. Add the tomatoes and cook gently for 15 minutes. Stir in chiles and cilantro. Add water and season to taste with salt and pepper.

In another large saucepan, combine the milk, cheeses, and butter. Cook over medium heat, stirring constantly, until melted and smooth. Add the cheese mixture to the tomato mixture. Cook over medium heat, stirring, just until soup comes to a boil. Serve immediately. *Makes 6 servings*

1/4 cup olive oil
1 onion, chopped
1 bunch green onions, chopped
3 cloves garlic, minced
2 pounds tomatoes, peeled and chopped
6 green Anaheim chiles, roasted, peeled, and cut into thin strips
1/2 cup cilantro, chopped
1 cup water
Salt and pepper
1 quart milk
2 cups shredded Monterey Jack cheese
1 cup shredded Colby cheese
1/4 pound (1 stick) butter

LOCKETT MEADOW MINESTRONE

The San Francisco Peaks north of Flagstaff offer year-round recreation, from skiing to hiking to a summertime chair lift ride. Lockett Meadow is a popular camping area during summer and fall, when wildflowers are scattered through the meadow and aspens shimmer green or gold. Bring along a thermos of this soup for a warming lunch.

Place the roast in a large pot and add water and bay leaves. Bring to a boil. Cover and simmer 3 hours, or until meat is tender. Remove meat from broth and add onions, carrots, and celery. Cook vegetables about 20 minutes, until tender. Cut the roast into bite-size pieces and add to broth and vegetables. Add tomatoes, tomato sauce, parsley, basil, garlic powder, green beans, peas, and kidney beans. Cook 15 minutes, until vegetables are done. Add pasta and heat thoroughly. Remove bay leaves and season to taste with salt and pepper. Garnish with grated Parmesan before serving.   *Makes 16 servings*

1 chuck roast, about 4 pounds
1 gallon water
4 bay leaves
2 onions, chopped
2 cups carrots, sliced
2 cups celery, sliced
1 (28-ounce) can diced tomatoes
1 (15-ounce) can tomato sauce
1/4 cup parsley, chopped
4 teaspoons dried basil
2 teaspoons garlic powder
2 (16-ounce) packages frozen green beans
1 (16-ounce) package frozen green peas
2 (15-ounce) cans kidney beans, drained
2 (16-ounce) packages spiral pasta,
   cooked and drained
Salt and pepper
Grated Parmesan cheese

FORT BOWIE BLACK BEAN SOUP

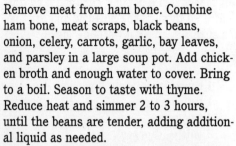

Remove meat from ham bone. Combine ham bone, meat scraps, black beans, onion, celery, carrots, garlic, bay leaves, and parsley in a large soup pot. Add chicken broth and enough water to cover. Bring to a boil. Season to taste with thyme. Reduce heat and simmer 2 to 3 hours, until the beans are tender, adding additional liquid as needed.

Cool, remove bay leaves, and purée the mixture in a blender. Return the soup to the pot and add red pepper flakes and cumin. Season with salt and heat until warmed through, stirring constantly so the soup doesn't stick. If the soup is too thick, add broth, a little at a time, to achieve desired consistency.

To serve, ladle into soup bowls and swirl 2 to 3 tablespoons of sour cream through each serving. If desired, garnish each bowl with a dollop of salsa.
Makes 8 to 10 servings

1 ham bone with $1/2$ pound of meat scraps
2 pounds dried black beans, sorted
  and rinsed
1 large onion
2 carrots, chopped
2 stalks celery, chopped
6 to 8 cloves garlic, minced
2 bay leaves
$1/2$ cup parsley, chopped
3 cups chicken broth
Thyme
3 to 4 teaspoons red pepper flakes
2 tablespoons ground cumin
Salt
16 ounces sour cream
Salsa, optional

SNOWBOWL STEAK SOUP

When winter rains arrive in the lower deserts, Arizona's mountaintops receive snow. Many skiers and snowboarders head north of Flagstaff to Arizona Snowbowl on the slopes of Mount Agassiz, one of Arizona's highest peaks. This hearty soup would make a welcome après ski dinner.

Combine broth, carrots, Worcestershire sauce, marjoram, rosemary, and 1/2 cup of the chopped onion in a Dutch oven. Cook until the carrots are soft. Season to taste with salt and pepper.

Sauté remaining 1/2 cup onion, mushrooms, parsley, garlic, and green bell pepper in butter until tender. Add sautéed vegetables to broth mixture. Bring broth mixture to a boil and add noodles. Cook 10 to 15 minutes, until noodles are tender.

Grill or broil steak until very rare. Cut into bite-size pieces. Add steak to soup and cook for several minutes longer to blend flavors. *Makes 10 to 12 servings*

5 quarts beef broth
1 cup carrots, chopped
1 tablespoon Worcestershire sauce
1/2 teaspoon dried marjoram
1/2 teaspoon dried rosemary
2 onions, chopped
Salt and pepper
1 pound mushrooms, sliced
1 cup parsley, chopped
3 cloves garlic, minced
1 green bell pepper, chopped
1/4 pound (1 stick) butter
1 (12-ounce) package noodles
1 sirloin steak, about 1 pound

GREETINGS from PETRIFIED FOREST ARIZ.

© J. R. WILLIS

MAIN DISHES

AJO CHICKEN

Some say the town of Ajo, the Spanish word for "garlic," was named for the desert lily, whose graceful white blossoms decorate the hillsides around the town of Ajo each spring. Native people used the lily's large bulb as a garlic-like seasoning and had countless uses for other desert plants as well. To learn more about ethnobotany, head for nearby Organ Pipe Cactus National Monument.

Preheat oven to 350 degrees F. Salt and pepper the chicken and place in a casserole dish. Melt 1/2 tablespoon of the butter in a skillet and sauté the mushrooms. Scatter the mushrooms over the chicken and pour 1/2 cup of the chicken broth over all. Cover and bake 10 minutes.

In the same skillet, melt the remaining 1 1/2 tablespoons butter and sauté the onion. Add chiles, garlic, and flour. Cook about 1 minute, stirring constantly. Remove chicken from oven and drain off pan drippings. Combine drippings with the remaining 1/2 cup chicken broth to equal 1 cup of liquid. Stir liquid into the onion mixture. Mix in yogurt and heat gently.

Spoon sauce over chicken and top with cheese. Bake another 15 minutes. Sprinkle with sunflower seeds before serving.
Makes 6 to 8 servings.

1 teaspoon salt
1/4 teaspoon pepper
2 chickens, cooked and boned
2 tablespoons butter
1/2 pound mushrooms
1 cup chicken broth
1 onion, chopped
2 (4-ounce) cans diced green chiles
4 cloves garlic, minced
1 tablespoon flour
1/2 cup plain yogurt
1 cup shredded Monterey Jack cheese
1/4 cup toasted sunflower seeds

KITT PEAK CHICKEN PISTACHIO

Thanks to a clear atmosphere and the dark-sky guidelines followed by many towns and cities, Arizona nights are studded with stars. West of Tucson, Kitt Peak National Observatory hosts nightly programs for stargazers. This chicken dish is studded with pistachios, a favorite Arizona crop.

Pound the chicken with a mallet to a quarter-inch thickness and season with pepper. Sauté chicken in oil for 2 to 3 minutes on each side. Add the orange juice, lemon juice, orange zest, and water. Cover and simmer 10 minutes, or until chicken is tender. Remove chicken.

Add green onions to pan and cook over medium heat until sauce is slightly thickened. Pour sauce over chicken and sprinkle with pistachios. *Makes 4 servings*

4 chicken breast halves, boned and skinl
1/8 teaspoon pepper
1 tablespoon vegetable oil
1/2 cup orange juice
2 tablespoons lemon juice
1/2 teaspoon orange zest, grated
2 tablespoons water
1/4 cup green onions, sliced
1/4 cup pistachios, chopped

FORT LOWELL CHICKEN WITH LIME

I had cast my lot with a soldier, and where he was, was home to me," wrote Martha Summerhayes, who lived at Tucson's Fort Lowell in 1878 with her husband. The fort's museum offers a look at the "glittering misery" of army life during Arizona's Apache Wars, 1861–1886, when the hardships of the frontier were lightened by the glamour of merry dinner parties.

Salt and pepper the chicken pieces. Heat oil in a large frying pan and sauté chicken until lightly browned, about 10 minutes. Cover, reduce heat, and cook about 10 minutes more. Remove the chicken and keep it warm. Drain the oil.

In the same pan, add the lime juice and heat on low until juice begins to bubble. Add butter, stirring until sauce is thick and opaque. Stir in the chives and dill weed. Spoon over chicken and serve. *Makes 6 servings*

1/2 teaspoon salt
1/2 teaspoon pepper
6 chicken breasts, boned and skinless
1/4 cup vegetable oil
Juice of 1 lime
1/4 pound (1 stick) butter
1/2 teaspoon chives, minced
1/2 teaspoon dill weed

QUARTZSITE MARGARITA CHICKEN

The population of this small desert community swells each winter when "snowbirds" flock here in RVs. The town is named for the rock (though the spelling differs), and rocks are the attraction every January and February when gem shows and swap meets turn the town into one large backyard bash. This festive version of grilled chicken will lend a party atmosphere to any occasion.

Mix the oil, lime juice, cilantro, tequila, and triple sec in a bowl. Add chicken and marinate 1 to 2 hours at room temperature or 4 hours in the refrigerator. Remove chicken and reserve marinade. Grill the chicken over hot coals 10 to 15 minutes, turning 3 or 4 times. Baste with reserved marinade. *Makes 4 servings*

2/3 cup olive oil
1/2 cup fresh lime juice
1/4 cup cilantro, chopped
1/4 cup tequila
1/8 cup triple sec
4 chicken breasts, boned and skinless

TORTILLA FLAT
ENCHILADA CASSEROLE

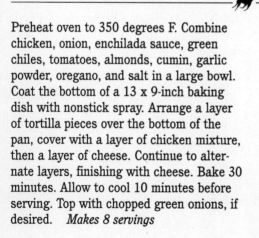

Preheat oven to 350 degrees F. Combine chicken, onion, enchilada sauce, green chiles, tomatoes, almonds, cumin, garlic powder, oregano, and salt in a large bowl. Coat the bottom of a 13 x 9-inch baking dish with nonstick spray. Arrange a layer of tortilla pieces over the bottom of the pan, cover with a layer of chicken mixture, then a layer of cheese. Continue to alternate layers, finishing with cheese. Bake 30 minutes. Allow to cool 10 minutes before serving. Top with chopped green onions, if desired. *Makes 8 servings*

6 to 8 boneless chicken breasts, cooked and cubed
3/4 cup onion, chopped
1 (15-ounce) can mild enchilada sauce
2 (4-ounce) cans diced green chiles
2 (10-ounce) cans diced tomatoes
1/2 cup almonds, sliced
1 teaspoon ground cumin
1 1/2 teaspoons garlic powder
2 teaspoons dried oregano
1/2 teaspoon salt
Tortilla pieces
3 cups shredded Monterey Jack cheese
Green onions, chopped (optional)

CHICKEN SIERRA ANCHA

Place the chicken pieces in a pot and add boiling salted water. Cook 45 minutes, adding more water as needed to cover chicken. Drain chicken, reserving the broth, and keep it warm.

Remove husks from tomatillos. Place half each of the tomatillos, cilantro, celery, green onions, lettuce, sunflower seeds, and chiles in a blender. Add 3/4 cup of the reserved chicken broth and blend well. Repeat with remaining half of ingredients plus another 3/4 cup broth.

Combine blended ingredients and mix in cumin and garlic powder. Heat the butter in a large skillet, add blended mixture, and simmer 15 minutes over low heat, stirring until thickened. Add more chicken broth if sauce gets too thick. Season to taste with salt.

Arrange chicken pieces on a platter and cover generously with the sauce. Garnish with chopped green onions, cilantro, or sunflower seeds. *Makes 4 servings*

1 chicken, about 3 pounds, cut into pieces
3 cups boiling salted water
1/2 pound tomatillos
1/2 bunch cilantro, roughly chopped
2 stalks celery, chopped
1 cup green onions, chopped
1 bunch leaf lettuce
1/4 cup sunflower seeds
3 canned green chiles
1/2 teaspoon ground cumin
1/2 teaspoon garlic powder
1 teaspoon butter
Salt
Additional green onions, cilantro, or sunflower seeds for garnish

SALT RIVER CILANTRO CHICKEN

Arizona claims to have more boats per capita than any other state in the United States. Northeast of Phoenix, a chain of four large reservoirs on the Salt River provide desert dwellers with places to float, fish, and swim. On the Upper Salt, whitewater enthusiasts will find a thrilling ride along a fifty-two-mile stretch that passes through starkly beautiful Salt River Canyon.

Mix oregano, garlic salt, pepper, and vinegar in a bowl and add the chicken pieces. Marinate 1 to 2 hours.

Heat oil in skillet. Add chopped onion and season to taste with paprika. Cook until onion is tender.

Place cilantro, quartered onion, tomatoes, and chile in a blender and purée. Add blended sauce to onion in skillet and cook another 2 minutes. Add chicken pieces and enough water to cover. Cook until chicken is tender, about 45 minutes.

Makes 4 servings

1 teaspoon dried oregano
1 tablespoon garlic salt
1 teaspoon pepper
2 tablespoons red wine vinegar
1 chicken, about 3 pounds, cut into pieces
2 tablespoons oil
1 onion, chopped
Paprika
1 bunch cilantro, roughly chopped
1 onion, quartered
2 medium tomatoes, chopped
1 yellow chile, seeded

CASA GRANDE CHICKEN CASSEROLE

Arizona has two places named Casa Grande, Spanish for large house. The first is a prehistoric Hohokam village, now a national monument. The newer Casa Grande is a farm town turned retirement community, with golf courses and winter homes. This casserole would be a hit at any community get-together.

Preheat oven to 350 degrees F. Combine lemon juice or vinegar with half-and-half and set aside to "sour."

Heat oil in a deep skillet to 375 degrees F. Fry the flour tortilla quarters on both sides, turning with tongs. Drain on paper towels.

Coat a 13 x 9-inch baking pan with non-stick spray. Spread enchilada sauce over the bottom of the pan. Place chicken pieces on top of the sauce. Use a spatula to cover the chicken with half-and-half. Scatter fried tortillas over the top and sprinkle with shredded cheese. Bake about 20 minutes, or until the cheese melts. Remove from oven and sprinkle with chopped jalapeños.   *Makes 6 to 8 servings*

1 teaspoon lemon juice or white vinegar
1 cup half-and-half
Oil for deep-frying
5 flour tortillas, quartered
1 (15-ounce can) green enchilada sauce
4 cups chicken, diced and cooked
2 cups shredded Cheddar cheese
2 tablespoons canned jalapeños, chopped

TOMBSTONE BEER-BASTED TURKEY STEAK

Rub turkey fillets with the seasoned salt.
Place in a shallow baking dish. Mix the
beer, brown sugar, pepper sauce, onion,
and oil. Season with salt and pepper. Pour
marinade over the turkey fillets, cover, and
refrigerate at least 4 hours. Remove turkey
and reserve marinade. Grill the turkey,
brushing with the reserved marinade. Cook
until the turkey is golden in color.
Makes 4 to 6 servings

8 turkey steak fillets
Seasoned salt
1 cup ale beer
1 tablespoon brown sugar
1/2 teaspoon hot pepper sauce
1 onion, chopped
1 tablespoon vegetable oil
Salt and pepper

SUNNYSLOPE SAUSAGE ENCHILADAS

Preheat oven to 350 degrees F. Brown
sausage and onion in a skillet. Pour off
excess fat. Beat eggs and add to sausage
mixture, scrambling them together. Soften
tortillas in microwave for 1 1/2 minutes. Put
some sausage mixture and a little cheese in
each tortilla and roll up, reserving some
cheese for garnish. Place seam side down in
a 13 x 9-inch baking dish coated with nonstick spray. Pour white sauce over the tortillas and sprinkle with additional cheese
and green chiles. Heat for 25 minutes.
Makes 4 servings

2 (12-ounce) packages sausage
1 large onion, chopped
4 eggs
12 fajita-size flour tortillas
1 pound Monterey Jack cheese, shredded
2 cups white sauce
1 (8-ounce) can diced green chiles

KINGMAN CROWN ROAST

When I-40 cut across northern Arizona, the reign of Route 66 ended. But turn off the freeway at Kingman, and you can drive the state's longest stretch of the Mother Road, where you'll find neon signs, roadside motels, and other vestiges of the past. When it comes to this pork roast, backyard barbecue kings rule.

Stir together onion, garlic, ginger, mustard, pepper, oil, bourbon, soy sauce, and vinegar in a bowl. Place roast in a heavy plastic bag, pour in the onion mixture, and seal. Tilt to coat the roast with marinade. Set bag in a deep pan and chill 4 to 24 hours.

Remove roast, reserving marinade. Grill over medium heat on an oiled grill, largest side down. Use a drip pan for the fat. Cover barbecue, open vents, and cook about 2 hours, basting frequently with the reserved marinade. Roast is done when a meat thermometer inserted at the bone in the thickest part of the roast reads 155 degrees F. *Makes 10 to 12 servings*

1 onion, chopped
2 cloves garlic, minced
2 tablespoons ginger, minced
1 teaspoon dry mustard
1/4 teaspoon pepper
1/2 cup olive oil
1/2 cup bourbon
1/2 cup soy sauce
2 tablespoons vinegar
1 pork crown roast with 12 ribs
   (about 7 pounds)

CROWN KING TEQUILA PORK CHOPS

Combine honey, soy sauce, tequila, vinegar, and Burgundy in a saucepan. Cook over low heat, stirring occasionally, until the sauce is smooth. Broil, bake, or pan-fry the pork chops, basting liberally with the sauce. Serve with any remaining sauce. *Makes 6 servings*

2 tablespoons honey
3 tablespoons soy sauce
4 tablespoons tequila
2 tablespoons rice vinegar
1/2 cup white Burgundy
6 pork chops

PUERCO RIVER PORK CHOPS

First-time visitors to Arizona are often surprised when the river indicated on a map is a dry, rocky gulch, or "wash." Puerco River cuts across colorful Petrified Forest National Monument in northeastern Arizona, and is dry as dust until sudden rainfall turns it into a muddy stream.

Rub the pork chops with Worcestershire sauce. Heat the olive oil in a large skillet over medium heat and brown chops without crowding. Drain any excess fat. Add water, cover, and simmer 10 minutes. Turn chops. Add capers and garbanzo beans. Simmer, covered, until meat is no longer pink at the bone, about 5 minutes. Season to taste with salt and pepper. *Makes 6 servings*

6 pork chops
2 tablespoons Worcestershire sauce
1 tablespoon olive oil
1/2 cup water
1 tablespoon capers, drained
1 (15-ounce) can garbanzo beans, drained
Salt and pepper

LAKE POWELL PORK AND GREEN CHILES

Heat oil in large skillet and sauté pork until brown. Drain off all but 1 tablespoon of fat. Add chopped chiles, garlic, onion, tomato, and water. Season with salt and pepper. Add cumin, cover tightly, and simmer 1 hour.   *Makes 4 servings*

2 tablespoons vegetable oil
1 pound lean pork, cubed
4 green Anaheim chiles, roasted, peeled, and chopped
3 cloves garlic, minced
1 onion, chopped
1 tomato, chopped
1 cup boiling water
Salt and pepper
1 teaspoon ground cumin

PAYSON PORK CHALUPAS

This town atop the 7,000-foot Mogollon Rim is known for outdoor escapes. Take a page out of one of Zane Grey's books and hike, fish, hunt, or explore the forests and streams of the rugged Rim Country around Payson. Before leaving for your adventures, start this hearty meal in a slow cooker and let its enticing scent welcome you on your return.

Place pork in a slow cooker and cover with water. Sort and rinse the pinto beans and add them to the cooker around the roast. Add garlic, bay leaves, salt, cumin, and chili powder. Cook on high 4 to 5 hours. Add salsa during the last 30 minutes of cooking time. Serve over corn chips, topped with sour cream.
Makes 4 to 6 servings

1 boneless pork butt
4 cups water
1 (16-ounce) package dried pinto beans
3 cloves garlic, minced
2 bay leaves
1 teaspoon salt
1 tablespoon ground cumin
1 tablespoon chili powder
1 tablespoon salsa
Corn chips
Sour cream

PAINTED DESERT PORK AND CHILE BURRITOS

Place pork in a Dutch oven. Add water and bring to a boil. Reduce heat and simmer, covered, until meat is half-cooked, about 35 minutes. Drain off water. Add onions, chiles, cilantro, tomatoes, garlic powder, salt, cumin, cloves, pepper, bay leaves, and jalapeño.

While meat is simmering, remove husks from tomatillos, cover with water, and bring to a boil. Drain and mash tomatillos. Add them to meat mixture and continue to simmer, stirring constantly, about 15 minutes. Add lemon juice. Blend cornstarch with 1 cup water. Stir into meat mixture and simmer another 15 minutes, stirring constantly.

Heat tortillas in a warm oven until softened. To make burritos, place a heaping 1/2 cup of meat mixture on a warm tortilla and sprinkle generously with shredded cheese. Fold sides in, then roll up. Reserve some cheese for garnish.
Makes 10 to 12 servings

3 pounds lean pork, cubed
1 gallon water
2 pounds onions, chopped
1 pound green chiles, chopped
1/2 bunch cilantro, chopped
2 tomatoes, chopped
1 teaspoon garlic powder
1 tablespoon salt
1 teaspoon cumin
1/2 teaspoon ground cloves
1/2 teaspoon pepper
2 bay leaves
1 jalapeño, chopped
1 pound tomatillos
Juice of 1/2 lemon
1/2 cup cornstarch
1 cup water
1 dozen tortillas
2 cups shredded Monterey Jack cheese

BUMBLEBEE HONEY AND BEER RIBS

This stop along a former stage route north of Phoenix was named for a misadventure shared by a group of prospectors in 1863. Out scouting for gold along creekside cliffs, they instead found a bee's nest glistening with golden honey. After being stung trying to retrieve the sweet treat, they referred to the site as Bumble Bee Creek.

Cut the spareribs into individual pieces. Mix beer, honey, sugar, mustard, chili powder, sage, lemon juice, salt, and pepper, blending thoroughly. Marinate the ribs in the sauce overnight. Remove ribs, reserving the marinade. Barbecue the ribs over a medium fire, turning every few minutes and basting frequently with the reserved marinade. Cook approximately 1 hour.
Makes 6 to 8 servings

6 pounds spareribs
3 cups beer
1 cup honey
1 teaspoon sugar
2 teaspoons dry mustard
1 teaspoon chili powder
1 teaspoon dried sage
2 tablespoons lemon juice
1 teaspoon salt
2 teaspoons pepper

DIAMONDBACKS BABY BACK RIBS

Combine the salt, black pepper, and 2 teaspoons of the red pepper flakes. Rub the seasonings all over the ribs and let stand 1 hour. Preheat oven to 400 degrees F.

Combine vinegar, butter, brown sugar, and the remaining 1 teaspoon of red pepper flakes in a saucepan and bring to a boil. Reduce heat and simmer 5 minutes. Set sauce aside and keep it warm.

Place ribs on a foil-lined baking pan and brown in the oven 15 minutes, turning once. Reduce oven temperature to 350 degrees F, baste the ribs with sauce, and continue baking them for 2 hours, basting occasionally with any remaining sauce and pan drippings.   *Makes 6 servings*

6 pounds baby back ribs
1 tablespoon salt
1 tablespoon freshly ground black pepper
3 teaspoons red pepper flakes
1 cup cider vinegar
1/4 pound (1 stick) butter
4 tablespoons brown sugar

TUCSON TAMALE PIE

Christmas means red and green—tamales, that is. Families throughout Arizona cele-brate the season by making tamales together, a labor of love. This casserole is much simpler to assemble, yet offers the traditional flavors of a red tamale.

Heat oil in skillet. Sauté onion and garlic until browned. Add ground beef and cook until browned. Add tomatoes, salt, pepper, cumin, and chili powder. Simmer on low heat 10 to 15 minutes. Set aside.

   Preheat oven to 425 degrees F. Follow package directions for Jiffy corn bread. Coat the bottom and sides of a casserole dish with nonstick spray. Spread two-thirds of the prepared corn bread batter over the bottom and sides of the pan. Pour in meat filling. Spread remaining corn bread batter over the top. Bake 30 to 35 minutes. Sprinkle with shredded cheese before serving.   *Makes 6 to 8 servings*

2 tablespoons vegetable oil
1 onion, chopped
3 cloves garlic, minced
1 1/2 pounds ground beef
1 (15-ounce) can diced tomatoes
2 teaspoons salt
1/4 teaspoon pepper
1 teaspoon ground cumin
4 teaspoons chili powder
1 package (8 1/2 ounce) Jiffy corn bread m
Shredded cheese

METEOR CRATER CHILI CON CARNE

Cook the suet and onion in a Dutch oven until the onion is tender but not browned. Add meat and brown. Mash together garlic and salt and stir into meat along with chili powder, cumin, and oregano. Add water. Cover and simmer for 1 hour. Add fried tor-tilla pieces and simmer another 30 to 40 minutes. Serve with shredded cheese.
Makes 6 to 8 servings

1/2 pound suet, coarsely ground
2 cups onions, chopped
3 pounds lean meat (beef, veal, and pork),
   coarsely ground
6 cloves garlic, minced
2 teaspoons salt
6 tablespoons chili powder
1 tablespoon ground cumin
1 tablespoon dried oregano
1 1/2 quarts water
1/4 cup tortilla pieces, fried
Shredded cheese

COCONINO CHUNKY CHILI

Within northern Arizona's vast Coconino National Forest, a town, county, plateau, and other places carry the name Coconino. "Coco" names derive from Cohonina, a prehistoric Indian culture that hunted game and gathered wild plants on the plateau country south of Grand Canyon. The cocoa powder in this chili is optional, a hint of Mexico's famous mole sauce.

Heat oil in a large Dutch oven. Sauté onion and garlic in oil until soft. Add beef and sausage. Cook until brown. Pour off fat. Add liquid from tomatoes. Chop the tomatoes and add to meat mixture. Add tomato sauce, chili powder, cumin, oregano, baked beans, salt, sugar, and if desired, 1 tablespoon unsweetened cocoa powder.

Simmer, partially covered, about 3 hours, stirring often. Stir in kidney beans and pinto beans. Cook another hour, until tender. At this point, the chili can be refrigerated a day or more. Serve with a selection of toppings, such as shredded cheese, sour cream, sliced black olives, chopped onions, and corn chips.   *Makes 18 to 20 servings*

4 tablespoons vegetable oil
2 large onions, chopped
4 cloves garlic, minced
4 pounds stew beef, cubed
3 pounds spicy sausage
2 (28-ounce) cans tomatoes
1 (15-ounce) can tomato sauce
6 tablespoons chili powder
3 tablespoons ground cumin
2 tablespoons dried oregano
2 (16-ounce) cans baked beans
2 teaspoons salt
2 tablespoons sugar
1 tablespoon unsweetened cocoa powder (optional)
2 (15-ounce) cans kidney beans
1 (15-ounce) can pinto beans
Additional toppings, such as shredded cheese, sour cream, sliced black olives, chopped onions, and corn chips.

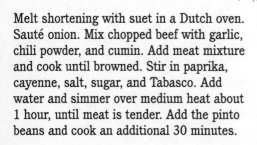

TEXAS CANYON TEX-MEX CHILI

Melt shortening with suet in a Dutch oven. Sauté onion. Mix chopped beef with garlic, chili powder, and cumin. Add meat mixture and cook until browned. Stir in paprika, cayenne, salt, sugar, and Tabasco. Add water and simmer over medium heat about 1 hour, until meat is tender. Add the pinto beans and cook an additional 30 minutes.

1 tablespoon shortening
1/2 pound suet, finely chopped
1 cup onion, chopped
2 pounds lean beef, chopped
3 cloves garlic, minced
1 1/2 tablespoons chili powder
1/2 tablespoon ground cumin
1 tablespoon paprika
1/2 teaspoon cayenne
1 teaspoon salt
2 tablespoons sugar
Dash of Tabasco
1 quart water
1 cup cooked pinto beans

NACO TACOS

Some say "Naco" combines the last letters in Arizona and Mexico because the town lies on the international border. Others believe it's an abbreviation for Nacozari, Mexico, a popular destination when Naco's train station was built in the 1800s. During Pancho Villa's rebellion in the early 1900s, this quiet border crossing near Douglas was a firestorm of flying bullets, homemade bombs, and barnstorming pilots.

Cook the meat in a skillet until browned, stirring to crumble. Season to taste with salt and pepper. Add cumin. Keep meat mixture warm while preparing taco shells.

Heat the lard in another skillet. Fry each tortilla until softened, then fold in half and cook on each side until crisp. Drain on paper towels. Fill each taco shell with a heaping tablespoon of meat. Add a few slices of onion, a generous amount of lettuce, and a tomato wedge, topping with shredded cheese. Serve with salsa and/or guacamole, if desired.
Makes 5 servings

1 pound lean ground beef
Salt and pepper
1/2 teaspoon ground cumin
1/2 cup lard
10 corn tortillas
1/2 onion, sliced
Shredded lettuce
1 tomato, cut in wedges
1 cup shredded cheese
Salsa
Guacamole

FREDONIA CHILI CON FRIJOLES

Heat oil in a Dutch oven. Sauté garlic until golden. Crumble in beef and cook 10 minutes, or until evenly browned. Pour some of the oil and drippings into a skillet and sauté onions and green peppers until tender. Add onions and pepper to cooked meat, along with tomatoes, kidney beans, tomato paste, chili powder, vinegar, cayenne, cloves, and bay leaf. Season to taste with salt and pepper. If desired, add sugar. Cover and simmer about 1 1/2 hours. If mixture is too dry, add additional tomatoes. If too liquid, uncover and simmer longer. *Makes 10 to 12 servings*

1/4 cup vegetable oil
3 cloves garlic, minced
4 pounds lean ground beef
6 onions, chopped
4 green bell peppers, chopped
3 (28-ounce) cans tomatoes
4 (15-ounce) cans kidney beans
2 (6-ounce) cans tomato paste
1/4 cup chili powder
1 teaspoon white vinegar
5 dashes cayenne
3 whole cloves
1 bay leaf
Salt and pepper
2 teaspoons sugar, optional

RILLITO BEEF BURRITOS

Combine the London broil, onion, and garlic in a skillet. Add enough water to cover. Season with garlic salt, salt, and pepper. Cover and cook until the meat is very tender, and the water has been absorbed. Pull the meat apart using two forks. Add tomatoes, chiles, and hot sauce. Simmer, uncovered, until liquids evaporate and meat mixture is just moist. Steam flour tortillas until hot. Spoon meat mixture onto tortillas and sprinkle with shredded cheese. Offer guests a variety of toppings.
Makes 8 servings

3 pounds London broil
1 large onion, chopped
4 cloves garlic, minced
Garlic salt
Salt and pepper
1 (28-ounce) can diced tomatoes
1 (7-ounce) can diced green chiles
1 (8-ounce) can hot tomato sauce
1 dozen flour tortillas
2 cups shredded Monterey Jack cheese
Additional toppings, such as sour cream, guacamole, chopped tomatoes, shredded lettuce

BISBEE BEER AND BEEF STEW

Numerous stairs wind up and down the hilly mining town of Bisbee, from Brewery Gulch to the old high school, built on a hillside with a ground-level door on each of its four floors. In October, the town hosts the Bisbee 1000, a staircase race. Competition is "steep," and everyone—winners, losers, and watchers—will prize this hearty stew.

Dredge stew meat in flour. Heat oil in a Dutch oven and brown meat with onions and garlic. Season with salt and pepper. Add the beer, soy sauce, Worcestershire sauce, steak sauce, bay leaves, thyme, and parsley. Cover and simmer 1 hour. Add potatoes and cook another 20 minutes, or until the potatoes are tender.
Makes 4 servings

- 1 pound chuck stew meat
- Flour for dredging
- 2 tablespoons vegetable oil
- 1 pound onions, chopped
- 3 cloves garlic, chopped
- Salt and pepper
- 12 ounces beer
- 1 tablespoon soy sauce
- 1 tablespoon Worcestershire sauce
- 1 tablespoon steak sauce
- 2 bay leaves
- 1 teaspoon dried thyme
- 2 tablespoons parsley, chopped
- 1 pound potatoes, chopped

LONDON BRIDGE BRISKET OF BEEF

Preheat oven to 350 degrees F. Place heavy-duty aluminum foil in the center of a large roasting pan. Sprinkle half the package of onion soup mix over the foil. Place brisket in the pan and sprinkle with the remaining soup mix. Seal the foil around the brisket. Bake 3 hours.

Combine brown sugar, cinnamon, pepper, ginger, lemon zest, lemon juice, honey, marmalade, brandy, Worcestershire sauce, and beer in a large bowl. Remove the meat from the oven, carefully turning back the foil to open. Pour the marinade mixture over the meat and reseal the foil. Return the meat to the oven. Place potatoes on oven rack. Bake another 60 to 75 minutes, or until meat is tender and potatoes are soft. *Makes 8 servings*

- 1 (1-ounce) packet onion soup mix
- 3 pounds lean beef brisket
- 2 tablespoons brown sugar
- 1 teaspoon cinnamon
- 1 teaspoon pepper
- 1 teaspoon ground ginger
- 1 tablespoon grated lemon zest
- 1 tablespoon lemon juice
- 1/4 cup honey
- 2 tablespoons orange marmalade
- 1 tablespoon brandy
- 1 teaspoon Worcestershire sauce
- 12 ounces beer
- 8 medium baking potatoes

JEROME GUACAMOLE BURGER

The town of Jerome perches on the side of Mingus Mountain, a former copper camp that nearly became a ghost town when the mines closed in 1953. Thanks to a dedicated historical society, the town's unique mixture of miners' shacks, Victorians, bungalows, and brick hotels has been preserved as private residences, shops, galleries, restaurants, and B&Bs.

Combine avocado, lemon juice, tomato, onion, garlic, salt, chili powder, and cayenne to make guacamole. Mix well and set aside.

Shape beef into four patties. Grill over hot coals, about 5 minutes on each side. Place each patty on a muffin half. Top with some guacamole and the other muffin half. Serve remaining guacamole on the side with corn chips. *Makes 4 servings*

3/4 cup ripe avocado, mashed
2 teaspoons lemon juice
3/4 cup tomato, chopped
1/4 cup onion, chopped
3 cloves garlic, crushed
1 teaspoon salt
1 teaspoon chili powder
Dash cayenne
1 pound ground beef
4 English muffins, split and toasted

GUNSIGHT SKEWERED BEEF

Combine tomato juice, vinegar, mustard, sugar, salt, and pepper in a shallow glass dish. Add the steak cubes. Cover and refrigerate about 2 hours. Remove meat and reserve marinade. Alternate the meat and vegetables on skewers. Grill 12 to 15 minutes, turning and basting with reserved marinade. *Makes 4 servings*

2 cups tomato juice
1/2 cup vinegar
1/4 cup prepared mustard
1 teaspoon sugar
1 teaspoon salt
1/2 teaspoon pepper
1 1/2 pounds sirloin, cut into 1-inch cubes
1/2 pound mushroom caps
1 green bell pepper, cut into 1-inch pieces
1 pint cherry tomatoes

SHOW LOW SHRIMP AND PEPPER CRISPS

Northern Arizona's Show Low got its name from a card game. Ranch partners decided to go their separate ways and settled the ranch's ownership with a deck of cards. After hours of play with no winner, they decided the one who showed low—drew the lowest card—would win. Deal these delectable crisps at your next party, and you'll win, too.

Preheat oven to 400 degrees F. Mix vegetable oil and butter. Soak tortillas in oil and butter for about 30 minutes. Place tortillas on several rimmed baking sheets and bake for 10 minutes. Remove tortillas from oven, and top with cheeses. Return to oven and bake until cheese melts.

In the meantime, heat olive oil in a large skillet on medium heat. Sauté garlic and peppers until peppers are crisp-tender, about 2 minutes. Add the shrimp and cook 3 to 4 minutes longer, until the shrimp are just cooked through. Remove from heat. Top each crisp with the shrimp and pepper mixture. *Makes 16 servings*

1/2 cup vegetable oil
1/2 cup butter, melted
16 corn tortillas
1/2 pound shredded Monterey Jack cheese
1/2 pound shredded Cheddar cheese
16 fresh jumbo shrimp, cleaned
1/2 cup olive oil
1 yellow bell pepper, cut into strips
2 green bell peppers, cut into strips
1 red bell pepper, cut into strips
3 cloves garlic, minced

ARCOSANTI AHI WITH CILANTRO

Toast the sesame seeds in a dry skillet over medium heat until golden and fragrant, stirring to prevent scorching. Set aside. Toss scallions, cilantro, and garlic together in a bowl. Add sesame seeds, sesame oil, honey, soy sauce, and Tabasco. Mix well. Place ahi in a flat dish. Pour marinade over ahi, cover with plastic wrap, and refrigerate 4 to 8 hours. Cook on the grill or broil 4 to 7 minutes on each side. *Makes 6 servings*

2 tablespoons sesame seeds
1 bunch scallions, sliced
1 cup cilantro, chopped
2 cloves garlic, crushed
1/4 cup plain sesame oil
1/4 cup honey
1/2 cup soy sauce
1 teaspoon Tabasco
3 pounds ahi tuna

TEMPLE BAR SNAPPER CASSEROLE

Arizona's large reservoirs are watery getaways for desert dwellers. On the Arizona side of Lake Mead, roughly midway between Hoover Dam and the western edge of Grand Canyon, Temple Bar boasts secluded coves and open waterways. The few residents who stay here year-round know their fish. Swap a few bites of this tasty casserole for the local lowdown on a favorite fishing spot.

Preheat oven to 350 degrees F. Dredge the fish fillets in seasoned flour. Melt the butter in a skillet and lightly sauté each fillet on both sides. Transfer to individual casserole dishes. Top each with a portion of chili sauce, then with shredded cheese. Bake 12 minutes. Sprinkle with parsley before serving. *Makes 6 servings*

6 pieces red snapper or other white fish (about 1 1/2 pounds)
1 cup flour, seasoned with salt and pepper
4 tablespoons (1/2 stick) butter
1 (7-ounce) can green chili sauce
3 cups shredded Monterey Jack cheese
1 tablespoon parsley, chopped

GRANITE DELLS GREEN ENCHILADAS

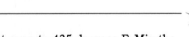

Preheat oven to 425 degrees F. Mix the flour and melted butter in a saucepan. Stir in broth and heat until mixture just bubbles but not boils. Add sour cream and chiles and set aside.

Heat oil in frying pan and dip in the tortillas to soften them. Sprinkle some cheese and onion in each tortilla and roll up. Arrange enchiladas in a baking dish. Pour green chili sauce over the top and bake 20 minutes. *Makes 4 to 6 servings*

1/4 cup flour
1/4 cup butter, melted
1 (10-ounce) can condensed chicken broth
1 cup sour cream
1 (4-ounce) can diced green chiles
Vegetable oil
12 corn tortillas
2 cups shredded Monterey Jack cheese
1 cup onion, finely chopped

GREEN VALLEY CHILE VERDE

Heat the oil in a Dutch oven. Sauté onions, garlic, jalapeños, and bell pepper for about 4 to 5 minutes over medium heat. Add chicken broth and simmer for 20 minutes, uncovered. Add potatoes and chiles and simmer another 30 minutes. Remove from heat and let stand for about 15 to 20 minutes, until the stew cools slightly. Stir in the half-and-half, mixing well. Reheat before serving, but do not allow to boil.

Makes 6 to 8 servings

3 tablespoons vegetable oil
2 onions, chopped
4 cloves garlic, chopped
2 jalapeños, chopped
1 green bell pepper, chopped
7 cups chicken broth
1 cups potatoes, diced
6 (4-ounce) cans diced green chiles
1 cup half-and-half

SAN RAFAEL CHILES RELLENOS

The San Rafael Valley, crossed by Coronado in 1540, has a rich ranching history. The valley's rolling, grassy hills have represented western plains and prairies in several movies, including Young Guns and Oklahoma! Today, the Empire/Cienega Resource Conservation Area preserves more than forty thousand acres of the valley's pristine grasslands, with the historic Empire Ranch at its heart.

Roast and peel the chiles. Cut a slit in each chile, remove the seeds, and stuff with cheese strips. Mix egg yolks, salt, milk, and 1/2 cup flour until smooth. Beat egg whites until firm but not dry. Fold whites into yolk mixture. Let stand for 10 minutes.

Meanwhile, dust the chiles with flour. Heat oil in a frying pan to 375 degrees F. Roll the chiles in the batter. Slide them into the hot oil, frying them two at a time until they are golden brown on all sides. Place cooked chiles on a serving dish and top with heated salsa or red chile sauce.

Makes 6 servings

6 mild green chiles

1/2 pound Monterey Jack cheese, cut into 1/2-inch strips

1/2 cup flour, plus additional flour for dredging

3 eggs, separated

1/2 teaspoon salt

1/2 cup milk

1 cup vegetable oil

Salsa or red chile sauce

SIDE DISHES

GARLAND PRAIRIE RICE

During the mid to late 1800s, wagons, stages, and mule trains crossed Garland Prairie near Williams, bringing settlers, supplies, and soldiers to Prescott's gold fields and Fort Whipple. This historic route, which can be hiked or biked, comes alive with wildflowers in late spring.

Preheat oven to 350 degrees F. In a large bowl, mix together the milk, parsley, peppers, onions, eggs, oil, and cheese, seasoning with salt and pepper. Add rice, mixing well, and pour into a casserole coated with nonstick cooking spray. Bake 45 minutes.
Makes 10 to 12 servings

6 cups cooked rice
2 cups milk
1 cup chopped fresh parsley
2 green bell peppers, chopped
1 cup chopped green onions, with tops
2 eggs, beaten
1/2 cup oil
2 cups shredded sharp Cheddar cheese
Salt and pepper

HUALAPAI JALAPEÑO RICE

In the Yuman language, "pai" means people. The Hualapai, or Pine Tree People, have lived at Grand Canyon's western reaches for centuries. Today, the Hualapai Nation offers driving and helicopter tours of Grand Canyon's remote western rim, as well as white- and smooth-water rafting.

Preheat oven to 350 degrees F. Combine the rice, sour cream, and jalapeños. Pour mixture into a casserole dish coated with nonstick cooking spray. Top with shredded cheese. Bake 20 minutes, or until cheese is melted and rice is heated through.
Serves 6 to 8

4 cups cooked rice
2 cups sour cream
1 (4-ounce) can diced jalapeños
1 cup shredded Cheddar cheese

MEXICAN RICE

Preheat oven to 350 degrees F. Heat oil or lard in a large skillet. Sauté onion and rice until lightly browned, about 10 minutes, stirring constantly.

In a large saucepan, combine the chicken broth, tomato juice, tomatoes, cilantro, garlic, salt, and pepper. Season to taste with cumin. Bring to a boil. Combine the broth mixture with the rice and transfer to a casserole dish. Cover and bake 25 to 30 minutes, until rice is fluffy.

Makes 6 to 8 servings

1/4 cup olive oil or melted lard
1 onion, chopped
2 cups long grain rice
2 cups chicken broth
1 cup tomato juice
1 cup tomatoes, diced
1 tablespoon cilantro, chopped
1 teaspoon garlic, minced
1 teaspoon salt
Pinch of ground white pepper
Ground cumin

K-TOWN CORN CASSEROLE

The Hopi town of Kykotsmovi, near Third Mesa, is known locally as K-Town. On the way to K-Town, you may see fields of corn growing in bushy hills. To most southwestern cultures, corn is a life-sustaining food with a spiritual element. For the Hopi, the growing season of corn is linked to the human cycles of life. Hopi villages celebrate the corn harvest every September. Serve this delicious dish at your next celebration.

Preheat oven to 350 degrees F. Melt the margarine over low heat. Add cream cheese and stir until melted. Add corn, onion, chiles, and salsa to cream cheese mixture. Season to taste with salt. Bake 35 minutes, uncovered, in a 2-quart casserole coated with nonstick cooking spray.

Makes 8 servings

1/4 pound (1 stick) margarine
1 (8-ounce) package cream cheese
1 (12-ounce package) frozen white corn, thawed
1/4 cup onion, chopped
1 (4-ounce) can diced green chiles
2 tablespoons hot salsa
Salt

WILLIAMS WILD RICE

The first Anglos to explore the territory of Arizona in the early 1800s were mountain men, rugged types who traveled along rivers trapping beaver and trading with Indians. One of the most famous of these wild men was scout, guide, and hunter Bill Williams, whose name graces a river, a mountain, and the town of Williams, where history buffs can drive or bike old Route 66, ride the Grand Canyon Railway, or hike the Overland Trail.

Thoroughly wash the rice and soak it in cold water for 2 hours. Drain, cover with boiling water, and boil 10 minutes. Drain the rice again.

Preheat oven to 350 degrees F. Melt butter in a large skillet and brown the drained rice. Add green pepper, mushrooms, onion, celery, tarragon, and half the salt and pepper. Cook 7 minutes, stirring frequently. Add the remaining salt and pepper and transfer rice to a baking dish coated with nonstick cooking spray. Place in a larger baking dish one-third full of hot water. Bake 1 hour.
Makes 4 to 6 servings

2 cups wild rice
1/2 cup butter
1 green bell pepper, finely chopped
1 cup mushrooms, chopped
1 onion, chopped
2 cups celery, chopped
1/4 teaspoon dried tarragon
1/2 tablespoon salt
1/4 teaspoon pepper

TWO GUNS TWICE-BAKED YAMS

Preheat oven to 400 degrees F. Rub each yam with vegetable oil. Bake until done, about 45 minutes. Allow to cool slightly. Cut away the top of each yam. Scoop out the insides and place in a bowl. Add maple syrup, margarine, cream, cinnamon, and nutmeg and beat together until fluffy. Spoon the mixture into the yam skins and bake another 15 minutes. *Makes 6 servings*

6 yams or sweet potatoes
Vegetable oil
1/4 cup maple syrup
1/4 pound (1 stick) margarine, melted
1/2 cup heavy whipping cream
1/2 teaspoon cinnamon
1/8 teaspoon nutmeg

PIPE SPRING NEW POTATOES

Mormon leader Brigham Young purchased this oasis on the Arizona Strip to graze and water the church's cattle herds. The stone house at Pipe Spring, built for self-sufficiency, featured a walled courtyard, gun ports, a dairy, and gardens. As a stop along the famed Honeymoon Trail, Pipe Spring sheltered many newlyweds making their way from the temple in St. George, Utah, to farming colonies in Arizona.

Cook the potatoes in boiling water until tender, about 20 minutes. Drain and set aside. Heat the butter and oil in a skillet. Add potatoes and sauté 8 to 10 minutes. Add garlic, salt, pepper, and Tabasco, reduce heat, and cook 3 to 4 minutes, or until the garlic turns golden brown.
Makes 4 to 6 servings

2 pounds small new potatoes
1/2 pound (2 sticks) butter
1 tablespoon vegetable oil
8 cloves garlic, minced
1 tablespoon salt
1 teaspoon freshly ground black pepper
1/2 teaspoon Tabasco

PRESCOTT COWPOKE BEANS

Historic Prescott, Arizona's first territorial capital, has an Old West feel, from its grassy town square and stately courthouse to the saloons of Whiskey Row. Every July, the nation's oldest rodeo rides into town, hot on the heels of other Western celebrations including Territorial Days, the Folk Arts Fair, a bluegrass music festival, and the Phippen Museum's annual Western art show and sale.

Sort and rinse the beans. Place all the ingredients in a large Dutch oven and add enough water to cover. Bring to a boil, then reduce heat. Cover and simmer at least 2 hours to blend flavors, adding more water as needed.   *Makes 8 to 12 servings*

2 pounds dried pinto beans
1 teaspoon cayenne
1/2 teaspoon Tabasco
1/2 cup chili powder
2 teaspoon salt
3 cloves garlic, minced
6 jalapeños, chopped
2 onions, chopped
1/2 pound bacon, chopped
1 (16-ounce) can diced tomatoes
1 teaspoon ground cumin
1 teaspoon dried marjoram
1 (12-ounce) can beer

ROUND VALLEY REFRITOS

Mash the beans with 1 cup of reserved liquid, using a potato masher or a food processor. Heat the bacon drippings in a large, heavy skillet. Sauté the onion and garlic until the onion is tender. Add the mashed beans, cumin, salt, black pepper, and red pepper flakes, stirring until the beans reach the desired consistency. Add more liquid if necessary. *Makes 6 servings*

4 cups cooked pinto beans, excess liquid drained and reserved
3 tablespoons bacon drippings
1 onion, chopped
3 cloves garlic, minced
1 teaspoon ground cumin
1 teaspoon salt
1 teaspoon ground black pepper
1 teaspoon red pepper flakes

CHUCK WAGON BEANS

Cut salt pork into four pieces. Place the pork pieces in a small pan, cover with water, and parboil 5 minutes.

Sort and rinse the beans. Place them in a large pot or Dutch oven and cover with water. Add cumin, garlic, and salt pork. Cover and simmer on low heat 1 1/2 to 2 hours, adding more water as needed. Stir in salt, pepper, and bacon drippings. Cook another 30 minutes, or until the beans are tender, stirring occasionally to prevent scorching. If desired, sprinkle with hot sauce before serving. *Makes 4 to 6 servings*

1/4 pound salt pork
1 pound dried pinto beans
6 cups water
1 teaspoon ground cumin
3 cloves garlic, minced
2 tablespoons salt
1/2 teaspoon pepper
2 tablespoons bacon drippings
Hot sauce

BRIGHT ANGEL BLACK BEANS

Bright Angel Trail, the most popular in Grand Canyon, hosts hundreds of hikers and mule riders daily. The trail descends more than nine miles to Bright Angel Creek, named for its clear waters by explorer John Wesley Powell. He'd already named a muddier Colorado River tributary the Dirty Devil, marking the contrast between beauty and danger on his 1869 journey into the unknown.

Sort and rinse the beans. Soak them overnight in a heavy pan with enough water to cover. Cut 1 onion and 1 green bell pepper in halves. Add onion and pepper halves to the beans and bring to a boil. Cover, reduce heat, and simmer 1 1/2 hours.

Meanwhile, heat oil or lard in a skillet. Chop the remaining onion and bell pepper and add to skillet with garlic. Sauté until onion is translucent and golden. Add cumin and bay leaf and cook 5 minutes, stirring constantly. Add tomato sauce and cook another 5 minutes. Cool slightly. Discard bay leaf and place mixture in a blender. Blend until smooth.

Remove onion and bell pepper halves from beans and discard. Add blended ingredients to beans. If sauce is too thick, add more water. Season to taste with salt. Simmer until flavors blend. Stir in wine vinegar and top with chopped onions before serving.   *Makes 4 to 6 servings*

1 pound dried black beans
2 onions
2 green bell peppers
5 tablespoons vegetable oil or melted lard
3 cloves garlic, minced
1 teaspoon ground cumin
1 bay leaf
1 (4-ounce) can tomato sauce
Salt
1 tablespoon wine vinegar
Chopped onions

KENTUCKY CAMP HUSHPUPPIES

During the latter nineteenth century, miners seeking their fortunes converged on Arizona Territory. Instead of riches, most found backbreaking work and loneliness. Kentucky Camp, now a historic site in Coronado National Forest, was named for a pair of prospectors from Kentucky. It could be they were the first to add a southwestern kick to this Deep South tradition.

Melt margarine in a skillet. Add onion, bell pepper, and jalapeños and sauté until tender. Transfer to a large bowl. Add flour, cornmeal, and corn. Mix well. Add enough buttermilk to achieve a pastry-like consistency. Heat oil to 375 degrees F. Drop batter by spoonfuls into hot oil and fry until golden brown on all sides. Drain on paper towels and serve immediately.
Makes 16 to 18

2 tablespoons margarine
1 cup onion, chopped
1 green bell pepper, chopped
2 jalapeños, chopped
1/2 cup self-rising flour
1 cup finely ground cornmeal
1 (8-ounce) can cream-style corn
Buttermilk
Vegetable oil for deep-frying

FOUR CORNERS JALAPEÑO CORN BREAD

Preheat oven to 375 degrees F. Melt the butter in a heavy 12-inch skillet and sauté jalapeños and onions until tender. Mix together eggs, milk, corn, onion, cornmeal, cheese, salt, soda, and flour in a large bowl. Stir in jalapeños and onion with any excess melted butter. Pour the batter into the prepared skillet. Bake 50 minutes, until brown.   *Makes 6 servings*

1/4 pound butter
3 jalapeños, finely chopped
1 cup onion, chopped
2 eggs, beaten
1 cup milk
1 (14.5-ounce) can cream-style corn
1 cup finely ground yellow cornmeal
1 cup shredded Cheddar cheese
1 teaspoon salt
1/2 teaspoon baking soda
5 tablespoons flour

HOPI BLUE CORN BREAD

Preheat oven to 400 degrees F. Mix flour, cornmeal, baking powder, salt, soda, and sugar in a large bowl. Stir in the eggs, buttermilk, and melted butter. Mix well with an electric mixer. Spoon the batter into a well-buttered 9-inch square pan and bake 30 to 40 minutes. When the corn bread looks done, cook another 5 minutes before removing from oven. Cool 5 minutes at room temperature before serving.
Makes 6 servings

1 1/4 cups white flour
1 1/4 cups blue cornmeal
2 1/2 teaspoons baking powder
1 teaspoon salt
1/2 teaspoon baking soda
3 tablespoons brown sugar
1 egg, beaten
1 2/3 cup buttermilk
1/3 cup melted butter

SPRINGERVILLE SKILLET CORN BREAD

Preheat oven to 350 degrees F. Combine cornmeal, flour, and baking soda in a large bowl. Blend in the buttermilk, eggs, sugar, honey, salt, and 1 cup of the milk. Mix thoroughly. Melt butter in a 10-inch skillet, swirling the pan to coat the sides. Pour the cornbread mixture into the skillet, forming an even surface. Pour the remaining 1 cup milk over the top. Bake, uncovered, about 50 minutes. Use a toothpick to test for doneness.   *Makes 4 to 6 servings*

1 1/3 cups yellow cornmeal
1/3 cup flour
1 1/2 teaspoons baking soda
1 cup buttermilk
2 eggs, beaten
1/3 cup sugar
1 teaspoon honey
2 cups milk
1 1/2 tablespoons butter

PUEBLO PEPPER-CORN MUFFINS

Preheat oven to 425 degrees F. Mix flour, cornmeal, baking powder, baking soda, and salt together in a large bowl. In a separate bowl, blend together the buttermilk, eggs, melted butter, bell pepper, and jalapeños. Add the liquid mixture to the dry ingredients and mix lightly. Spoon the batter into a buttered muffin tin, filling the cups two-thirds full. Bake 18 to 20 minutes.
Makes 12

1 cup flour
1 cup cornmeal
2 teaspoons baking powder
1 teaspoon baking soda
1/2 teaspoon salt
1 cup buttermilk
2 eggs, beaten
4 tablespoons butter, melted
1 red bell pepper, chopped
4 jalapeños, chopped

BLUE RIVER BLUEBERRY MUFFINS

Preheat oven to 350 degrees F. Coat muffin tins with nonstick cooking spray. Combine milk and lemon juice. Set aside. Cream together the margarine and sugar in a large bowl. Stir in eggs. Combine flour, baking powder, and salt. Alternately add dry ingredients and milk to the creamed mixture, stirring after each addition. Lightly mix in pecans, lemon zest, and blueberries. Bake 30 to 40 minutes. When done, dip muffin tops in melted butter and then sugar.   *Makes about 2 dozen*

1/2 cup milk
1/4 cup lemon juice
1 1/2 sticks margarine, softened
1 1/4 cups sugar
3 eggs
2 cups flour
2 teaspoons baking powder
1 teaspoon salt
3/4 cup pecans, chopped
2 teaspoons grated lemon zest
1 cup blueberries
1/2 cup butter, melted
1/4 cup sugar

RAMSEY CANYON CORN BREAD

This riparian area in southeastern Arizona is a favorite destination for birders. Over a dozen species of hummingbirds visit here, along with wild parakeets, trogans, and other interesting avians. The Ramsey Canyon Preserve, nearly four hundred acres, is one of six Nature Conservancy sites in Arizona open to the public.

Preheat oven to 325 degrees F. Mix flour, cornmeal, baking powder, and salt in a large bowl. Combine butter, sugar, and eggs in a separate bowl. Stir in chiles, corn, and cheeses. Add liquid mixture to dry ingredients, mixing lightly, and pour into a 11 x 9-inch pan coated with nonstick cooking spray. Bake 1 hour.
Makes 10 servings

1 cup flour
1 cup yellow cornmeal
4 teaspoons baking powder
1/4 teaspoon salt
1/2 pound (2 sticks) butter, melted
1 cup sugar
3 eggs
1 (4-ounce) can diced green chiles
1 (15-ounce) can cream-style corn
1 cup shredded Monterey Jack cheese
1 cup shredded Cheddar cheese

MULESHOE RANCH APPLE MUFFINS

Preheat oven to 325 degrees F. Coat muffin tin with nonstick cooking spray. Combine white sugar and butter in a small bowl, mixing until crumbly. Set aside for topping.

Combine brown sugar, oil, and egg in a large bowl. In a separate bowl, combine buttermilk, soda, salt, and vanilla. Alternately add flour and buttermilk mixture to egg mixture, stirring after each addition. Fold in apples and walnuts. Spoon batter into muffin tin. Sprinkle with topping. Bake 30 minutes. *Makes 12*

$1/3$ cup white sugar
1 tablespoon butter
1 $1/2$ cups firmly packed brown sugar
$2/3$ cup vegetable oil
1 egg
1 cup buttermilk
1 teaspoon baking soda
1 teaspoon salt
1 teaspoon vanilla
1 $1/2$ cups flour
1 $1/2$ cups apples, peeled and chopped
$1/2$ cup walnuts, chopped

TUBAC BANANA-ZUCCHINI BREAD

Forty-five miles south of present-day Tucson, Spanish colonists established the Presidio San Ignacio de Tubac in 1752. Tubac was abandoned and resettled at least three times by Spain, Mexico, and the United States. In 1860 Tubac was the largest town in Arizona Territory. Today, Tubac is a lively arts village, and Tubac Presidio State Park preserves the area's rich past.

Preheat oven to 350 degrees F. Mix flour, soda, salt, cinnamon, and baking powder in a bowl. Combine the oil, eggs, sugar, vanilla, and banana extract in a large bowl. Stir in the zucchini and bananas, mixing well. Add the dry ingredients to the wet ingredients, stirring until moistened. Fold in nuts. Pour into two buttered and floured 8 1/2 x 4 1/2-inch loaf pans. Bake 1 hour.
Makes 2 loaves

3 cups flour
1 teaspoon baking soda
1 teaspoon salt
1 teaspoon cinnamon
1/2 teaspoon baking powder
1 cup vegetable oil
3 eggs
2 cups sugar
1 tablespoon vanilla
1 teaspoon banana extract
2 cups zucchini, shredded
2 cups bananas, mashed
1 cup walnuts or pecans, chopped

WHISKEY ROW BREW BREAD

In the early 1900s, Arizona was still the wild and woolly West. Whiskey Row in Prescott boasted forty saloons, and a cowboy could drink his way from one end of the row to the other. Whiskey was imported from more civilized parts, but beer was brewed locally. Use your local brew to stir up these biscuits, an old cowboy favorite.

Preheat oven to 350 degrees F. Mix egg and molasses in a large bowl. Stir in flour. Slowly stir in the beer. Mix with a wooden spoon until blended. Pour batter into an 8 1/2 x 4 1/2-inch loaf pan coated with nonstick cooking spray. Bake 45 to 50 minutes, or until bread sounds hollow when thumped.   *Makes 1 loaf*

2 large eggs
1/4 cup molasses
2 1/2 cups self-rising flour
12 ounces dark beer

COWBOY COFFEE CAKE

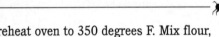

Preheat oven to 350 degrees F. Mix flour, salt, sugars, ginger, and 1 teaspoon of the cinnamon in a large bowl. Mix in oil. Transfer 1 cup of this mixture to another bowl to make topping. To this, add walnuts and the remaining 1 teaspoon of cinnamon. Set aside.

To the original mixture, add baking soda, baking powder, egg, and buttermilk. Mix and pour into a 13 x 9-inch baking pan coated with nonstick cooking spray. Sprinkle topping evenly over the batter. Bake 40 to 45 minutes.
Makes 8 to 10 servings

2 1/4 cups flour
1/2 teaspoon salt
1 cup brown sugar
3/4 cup white sugar
1/4 teaspoon powdered ginger
2 teaspoons cinnamon
3/4 cup vegetable oil
1 cup walnuts
1 teaspoon baking soda
1 teaspoon baking powder
1 egg, beaten
1 cup buttermilk

Greetings from WILLIAMS ARIZ.

GATEWAY TO GRAND CANYON

SAUCES, SALSAS & CONDIMENTS

LUKACHUKAI CHILI SAUCE

The Lukachukai mountain range lies along the Arizona–New Mexico border. Drive south along Highway 191 from Rock Point, and you'll see reddish cliffs of wind-carved Wingate Sandstone give way to the rugged Lukachukais, where Tony Hillerman's detective Joe Leaphorn solves a mystery in *The Blessingway*.

Melt the shortening in a saucepan. Stir in the flour and cook 1 minute, stirring. Add the chili powder and 1/2 cup of the stock. Cook 1 minute longer. Add the salt, garlic powder, oregano, coriander, cumin, and remaining 1 1/2 cups stock. Simmer about 10 minutes.   *Makes 2 cups*

2 tablespoons shortening
2 tablespoons flour
1/4 cup chili powder
2 cups chicken stock
3 teaspoons salt
1 teaspoon garlic powder
1 teaspoon dried oregano
1/2 teaspoon ground coriander
1 teaspoon ground cumin

GANADO RED CHILE SAUCE

At Hubbell Trading Post National Historic Site near Ganado, Navajo weavers demonstrate the artistry and skill of traditional rug-making. Various regions of the reservation are associated with particular weaving styles. Ganado weavers are known for using a deep red yarn to make a rug with a traditional diamond-shaped central design.

Rinse seeds from the chipotles. Chop the chipotles finely. Peel the tomatoes and process in a blender or food processor. Heat the oil in a saucepan. Stir in chipotles, tomatoes, onion, garlic, cumin, and oregano. Simmer 15 to 20 minutes. Cool to room temperature before serving.
Makes about 2 cups

1 (3-ounce) can chipotles
1 pound ripe tomatoes
3 tablespoons peanut oil
1 onion, chopped
3 cloves garlic, minced
1 teaspoon ground cumin
1 teaspoon dried oregano

GATES PASS GREEN CHILE SAUCE

Heat the oil in a large skillet. Sauté the onion and garlic. Stir in the flour and cumin. Cook 3 minutes, stirring constantly. Reduce heat and add broth, green chiles, jalapeños, oregano, and salt. Continue cooking about 25 minutes, until thickened. *Makes about 1 cup*

1/4 cup olive oil
1/2 cup onion, chopped
3 cloves garlic, minced
2 tablespoons flour
1 teaspoon ground cumin
1 1/2 cups chicken broth
1 cup green chiles, diced
1 tablespoon jalapeños, chopped
1/4 teaspoon oregano
1 teaspoon salt

APACHE TRAIL ENCHILADA SAUCE

Heat the olive oil in a saucepan. Add flour and stir until browned. Add the chili powder, broth, and garlic powder. Mix well and bring to a boil. Reduce heat and simmer 15 minutes.   *Makes 2 1/2 cups*

1/4 cup olive oil
1/4 cup flour
1/3 cup chili powder
2 cups beef broth
1/2 teaspoon garlic powder

STAGECOACH GREEN ENCHILADA SAUCE

Heat the oil in a skillet. Sauté the onion, garlic, and jalapeño until the onion is tender. Add chiles, half-and-half, and salt. Simmer for a few minutes, or until sauce is thick.   *Makes 2 3/4 cups*

2 tablespoons vegetable oil
1 onion, chopped
3 cloves garlic, minced
1 jalapeño, chopped
3 (4-ounce) cans diced green chiles
1 cup half-and-half
1/4 teaspoon salt

MONUMENT VALLEY SALSA VERDE

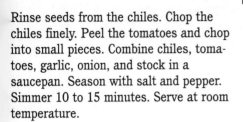

Rinse seeds from the chiles. Chop the chiles finely. Peel the tomatoes and chop into small pieces. Combine chiles, tomatoes, garlic, onion, and stock in a saucepan. Season with salt and pepper. Simmer 10 to 15 minutes. Serve at room temperature.

1 (8-ounce) can serrano chiles, chopped
1 pound green tomatoes, peeled
  and chopped
3 cloves garlic, minced
1 onion, diced
2 cups chicken stock
Salt and pepper

HAVASUPAI SALSA FRESCA

The People of the Blue-Green Water, the Havasupai, live in Havasu Canyon at the western end of Grand Canyon. Havasu Creek tumbles from cliffs in several spectacular waterfalls, splashing into travertine-lined pools that reflect turquoise skies. An eight-mile trail leads to Supai Village, where hikers and backpackers can enjoy this paradise.

Mix tomatoes, lemon juice, cilantro, olives, onions, garlic, olive oil, chiles, and jalapeño in a large bowl. Refrigerate before serving.   *Makes about 5 cups*

4 cups tomatoes, chopped
1/3 cup lemon juice
1/3 cup cilantro, chopped
1/4 cup ripe olives, chopped
4 green onions, chopped
4 cloves garlic, finely chopped
1 tablespoon olive oil
1 (4-ounce) can diced green chiles
1/2 jalapeño, finely chopped

TRADING POST TACO SAUCE

Combine tomato paste, crushed red chile, vinegar, salt, garlic powder, and oregano. Refrigerate 2 hours before using.
Makes 1 cup

1 (6-ounce) can tomato paste
1 tablespoon crushed red pepper flakes
1/4 cup white vinegar
1 teaspoon salt
1 teaspoon garlic powder
Pinch of dried oregano

HASH KNIFE HOT SAUCE

During the late 1800s, the Aztec Land and Cattle Company ran sixty thousand head on two million acres in northern Arizona, the third largest cattle operation in North America. The Hash Knife outfit, mostly from Texas, had a reputation for toughness, a helpful trait for dealing with rustlers, rough country, and harsh weather. Cowboy up and try this hot sauce, which packs a dozen jalapeños.

Rinse seeds from jalapeños. Chop the jalapeños very finely. Add garlic, salt, and lemon juice. Mix well before serving. Serve with chips and a fresh salsa.
Makes about 1 cup

12 canned jalapeños, seeded and chopped
3 cloves garlic, chopped
1/4 teaspoon salt
1 tablespoon lemon juice

BULLHEAD CITY BARBECUE SAUCE

There's a hint of fire in this barbecue sauce, hot as a Bullhead City summer, when temperatures often top the Arizona charts, reaching the hundred-teens. Locals beat the heat by floating, fishing, and playing in the waters of the Colorado River ... or in the air-conditioned casinos across the river at Laughlin, Nevada.

Combine all ingredients in a saucepan and simmer 30 to 40 minutes. Use the sauce to baste meat while grilling.
Makes about 1 cup

1/4 cup vegetable oil
1 (8-ounce) can tomato sauce
1 teaspoon paprika
1/2 teaspoon powdered ginger
1/2 teaspoon garlic powder
1 teaspoon chili powder
1/4 teaspoon cayenne
Dash Tabasco sauce

DESERT CITRUS BARBECUE SAUCE

Combine orange juice, water, vinegar, honey, chili powder, brown sugar, salt, and pepper in a jar. Cover tightly. Shake well before using on pork or chicken.
Makes about 2 1/2 cups

1 cup fresh orange juice
1/2 cup water
1/2 cup red wine vinegar
1/4 cup honey
1 teaspoon chili powder
1/3 cup firmly packed brown sugar
1/2 teaspoon salt
1/2 teaspoon freshly ground black pepper

V-BAR-V BARBECUE SAUCE

This former ranch along Beaver Creek, now a heritage site, was acquired by the forest service in 1994 in order to protect petroglyphs made by Sinagua Indians nine hundred years ago. During the early 1900s, the V-Bar-V became a dude ranch, where visitors enjoyed trail rides, swimming holes, and cookouts. Try this spicy sauce at your next cookout.

Heat oil in a skillet. Sauté onion in oil, then add garlic and cook until tender. Add ketchup, vinegar, lemon juice, Worcestershire sauce, brown sugar, chili powder, celery seed, cumin, and mustard, mixing well. Simmer 30 minutes, uncovered. *Makes about 3 cups*

1/4 cup olive oil
1 onion, finely chopped
4 cloves garlic, finely chopped
1 cup ketchup
1/2 cup red wine vinegar
1/3 cup lemon juice
1/4 cup Worcestershire sauce
1/4 cup firmly packed brown sugar
4 teaspoons chili powder
2 teaspoons celery seed
1 teaspoon ground cumin
2 teaspoons dry mustard

LA POSADA BÉARNAISE

A visit to Winslow's lovingly restored La Posada Hotel is a trip back in time, when travelers dined in the efficient yet elegant Harvey Houses along the Santa Fe rail line. Wander down the many-windowed orangerie or stroll among the rose garden and imagine white-aproned Harvey Girls being wooed by local cowboys. Fred Harvey himself would have approved of this creamy béarnaise.

Heat water in the bottom pan of a double boiler. Mix vinegar, onion, tarragon, and pepper in the top of a double boiler. Place the pan directly on the heat and boil until liquid is reduced by half. Insert the pan into the bottom of the double boiler. Whisk in egg yolks, stirring constantly, until thickened. Stir in butter, a little at a time, until sauce is smooth and thick. Stir in parsley before serving. *Makes about 1 cup*

1/4 cup red wine vinegar
2 teaspoons onion, finely chopped
1 1/2 teaspoons tarragon, chopped
1/8 teaspoon freshly ground black pepper
4 egg yolks
1 stick plus 4 tablespoons butter, softened
1 tablespoon parsley, chopped

FORT HUACHUCA CHILI BUTTER

Place butter, salt, chili powder, garlic, and lemon juice in a blender and process until smooth. *Makes 3/4 cup*

1/4 pound (1 stick) butter, softened
1 teaspoon salt
1 tablespoon chili powder
2 cloves garlic, minced
1/4 cup lemon juice

HARQUA HALA JALAPEÑO JELLY

The name "Harqua Hala" has been given to a mountain range, peak, and a late-1800s mining camp. It comes from the Mohave word for running water, "Ah-ha-quahla," referring to a dependable spring in the mountains. And though it might be instinctive to reach for water to quench a chile-induced fire, experienced "chile heads" know to reach for milk or bread instead.

Mix the bell pepper, jalapeños, sugar, and vinegar in a saucepan and bring to a rolling boil. Boil about a minute. Remove from heat and cool slightly. Add the pectin and food coloring. Mix well. Strain into hot, sterilized jars and seal. Serve over a block of cream cheese with crackers on the side. *Makes about 8 cups*

1 large green bell pepper, seeded and grou
4 jalapeños, seeded and ground
6 cups sugar
1 1/2 cups cider vinegar
1 (6-ounce) bottle liquid pectin
5 or 6 drops green food coloring

SANTA CRUZ CRANBERRY RELISH

Preheat oven to 350 degrees F. Mix cranberries and sugar and spread on a foil-lined cookie sheet. Bake 1 hour. Spread the walnuts on another cookie sheet and bake 10 minutes to toast. Mix the orange marmalade and lemon juice in a bowl. Add the cranberries and nuts. Cover and refrigerate before serving. *Makes 4 to 5 cups*

1 bag fresh cranberries
1 1/2 cups sugar
1 cup walnuts, chopped
1 cup orange marmalade
1/4 cup fresh lemon juice

SHIVA TEMPLE INDIAN RELISH

Inside Grand Canyon are towering rock formations, many named by Clarence Dutton, who explored the canyon with Powell in 1872 and later for the U.S. Geological Survey. To reflect the canyon's grandeur, Dutton chose names from Eastern mythic and religious traditions, such as Shiva Temple, which stands near the North Rim. You'll "relish" this taste of the East whenever you have a surplus of green tomatoes.

Coarsely grind the tomatoes, bell peppers, and cabbage in batches, using the metal blade of a food processor. Sprinkle with salt and allow to stand overnight. Rinse the mixture well and drain. Place in large saucepan and add the sugar, mustard seed, turmeric, vinegar, celery seed, and water. Heat to boiling and cook 3 minutes. Seal in hot, sterilized jars and process 10 minutes.
Makes 20 cups

- 10 green tomatoes
- 12 green bell peppers
- 6 red bell peppers
- 4 cups shredded cabbage
- 1/2 cup salt
- 6 cups sugar
- 2 tablespoons mustard seed
- 1 1/2 teaspoons turmeric
- 4 cups cider vinegar
- 1 tablespoon celery seed
- 2 cups water

HI JOLLY HOT PEPPER JELLY

In 1857, the U.S. Army imported camels from the Middle East to see how they would fare in the high desert. The camels came with their own handler, Hadj Ali—"Hi Jolly" to the soldiers, who couldn't pronounce his name. The camels trekked from Texas to California and back, but Congress ignored the Secretary of War's urgings to order another thousand. Hi Jolly returned to Arizona, keeping a few camels for an unsuccessful freighting venture before releasing them into the desert. A memorial to Hi Jolly stands in Quartzsite, where he lived before his death in 1902.

Blend the chiles, bell pepper, and vinegar in a blender. Pour into a saucepan and stir in the sugar. Bring to a boil and stir in the food coloring. Skim foam and add the pectin. Cook, stirring constantly, for 2 minutes. Remove from heat and pour into sterilized jars. Seal with paraffin.
Makes about 4 pints

- 1 cup Anaheim, poblano, or other chiles, chopped
- 1 green bell pepper, chopped
- 1 1/4 cups red wine vinegar
- 6 cups sugar
- 3 drops green food coloring
- 1 (6-ounce) jar liquid pectin

Greetings from WINSLOW ARIZ

DESSERTS

SLEEPING BEAUTY SOPAIPILLAS

The Sleeping Beauty Mine near Globe is one of few Arizona turquoise mines still producing today. Sleeping Beauty turquoise is a pure sky-blue without matrix (veins). While turquoise jewelry goes in and out of fashion everywhere else, southwesterners have adorned themselves with this beautiful stone since prehistoric times.

Combine flour, salt, and baking powder in a deep bowl. Mix in the shortening until blended. Add water and mix well. Turn dough out onto a lightly floured board. Knead until smooth, about 2 minutes. Roll the dough into a ball. Cover and refrigerate 20 minutes.

2 cups flour
1/4 teaspoon salt
1 1/2 teaspoons baking powder
4 tablespoons shortening
3/4 cup water
3 cups oil for deep-frying
1/2 cup sugar
Honey

Cut dough in half, forming two balls. Roll the first ball into a 12-inch square on a lightly floured board. Cut into 3-inch squares. Repeat with the remaining dough. Heat the oil in a deep skillet or fryer to 375 degrees F. Fry sopaipillas two at a time, 25 seconds on each side, or until golden brown. Remove with a slotted spoon and drain on paper towels. Sprinkle with sugar and serve with honey.
Makes 32

SNOWFLAKE FRIED ICE CREAM

Scoop out 4 to 5 balls of ice cream. Return them to the freezer. Mix cookie crumbs, cinnamon, and sugar. Roll the ice cream balls in half the crumb mixture and freeze them again until firm. Dip ice cream balls in beaten egg, then roll again in the remaining crumbs. Freeze until ready to use.

1 pint vanilla ice cream
1/2 cup crushed cookie crumbs
1 teaspoon cinnamon
2 teaspoons sugar
1 egg, beaten
Oil for deep-frying
Whipped cream
Honey

Heat the oil to 350 degrees F in a deep fryer. Place ice cream balls, one at a time, in the fryer basket and cook each for 1 minute. Immediately transfer to a serving dish. Drizzle with honey, top with whipped cream, and serve.   *Makes 4 to 5 servings*

PATAGONIA RICE PUDDING

Combine the rice, water, cinnamon stick, orange zest, and salt in a large saucepan. Bring to a boil, then reduce heat and cook, covered, until most of the water is absorbed. Stir in milk and sugar. Cook over low heat, stirring constantly, until mixture thickens. Add the raisins and vanilla and cook 2 minutes more. Remove from heat and let cool slightly. Sprinkle lightly with ground cinnamon before serving.
Makes 6 servings

1 cup long grain white rice
3 cups water
1 stick cinnamon
1 tablespoon orange zest
Pinch of salt
4 cups milk
1 1/2 cups sugar
1/2 cup raisins
1 teaspoon vanilla
Ground cinnamon

BUTTERFIELD STAGE BANANAS FLAMBÉ

Preheat oven to 425 degrees F. Generously coat a baking dish with 1 tablespoon of the butter. Sprinkle with 3 tablespoons of the brown sugar. Cut the bananas in half lengthwise and arrange cut side down in the baking dish. Sprinkle with remaining brown sugar and dot with remaining butter. Bake 6 to 10 minutes, or until the sugar melts and the bananas turn brown. Remove from oven, add rum, and ignite. Serve hot with ice cream.
Makes 6 servings

2 tablespoons butter
6 tablespoons brown sugar
6 ripe bananas, peeled
1/4 cup dark rum
Vanilla ice cream

FLORENCE MOLDED FLAN

Florence hosts a historic home tour every February. More than a hundred of the town's buildings are on the National Historic Register. At the red brick courthouse, time stands still. Because the town ran out of funds before a clock could be purchased, locals painted on a clock face that will forever read quarter past eleven. This elegant dessert is timeless, too.

Mix 1/2 cup of the sugar with water in a saucepan. Cook over medium heat, stirring until the sugar melts and forms a light brown syrup. Pour the syrup into a 6-cup ring mold. Tip the mold from side to side, coating the bottom with syrup. Place in the refrigerator to cool.

Preheat the oven to 350 degrees F. Pour the milk into a saucepan with the vanilla bean and cook over medium heat until the milk comes to a boil. Remove the vanilla bean and discard it. Remove milk from heat and allow to cool slightly.

Meanwhile, beat the eggs and the remaining 1/2 cup sugar with an electric mixer until smooth. Slowly pour egg mixture into hot milk, stirring constantly. Pour the custard into the prepared mold. Fill a shallow pan with 1 1/2 inches of hot water. Set the custard mold in the pan of water and place both in the oven. Bake 50 to 60 minutes, until set. Cool, then refrigerate at least 3 hours before serving.

Makes 6 to 8 servings

1 cup sugar
3 tablespoons water
5 cups milk
1 vanilla bean, slit
6 eggs

YUMA MOCHA FREEZE

One of Arizona's earliest settlements, Yuma lies along the Colorado River at an elevation below 200 feet. Summers are wickedly hot, and one tall tale has it that a soldier stationed there in the 1850s died, went to hell, then sent for his blankets from Yuma because he'd become so accustomed to the heat. If only he'd tried this heavenly dessert instead.

Dissolve instant coffee in water in a small bowl. Set aside. Combine cookie crumbs, 1/2 cup of the pecans, and butter. Pat into the bottom of a 13 x 9 x 2-inch pan to form a crust. Beat the cream cheese until it is light and fluffy. Blend in coffee, condensed milk, and chocolate syrup. Fold in whipped topping and spread over crust. Sprinkle the remaining 1/4 cup pecans over the top. Freeze until firm. *Makes 24 servings*

2 teaspoons instant coffee granules
1 tablespoon hot water
1 cup crumbs made from cream-filled chocolate sandwich cookies
3/4 cup pecans, chopped
1/4 cup butter, melted
2 (8-ounce) packages cream cheese, softened
1 (14-ounce) can sweetened condensed milk
1/2 cup chocolate syrup
1 (8-ounce) carton frozen whipped topping, thawed

MARIACHI MARGARITA PIE

Mix the gelatin with 1/2 cup of the sugar and salt in a saucepan. Beat together the egg yolks and lime juice and add to saucepan with gelatin mixture. Cook over low heat, stirring constantly, until gelatin is dissolved, 5 to 7 minutes. Remove from heat and stir in lime zest, tequila, and Triple Sec. Chill until mixture mounds slightly when dropped from a spoon. Beat egg whites with remaining 1/2 cup sugar until stiff. Fold the egg whites into the lime mixture and pour into the prepared pie shell. Refrigerate until firm.
Makes 6 to 8 servings

1 (1-ounce) packet unflavored gelatin
1 cup sugar
1/2 teaspoon salt
4 eggs, separated
1/2 cup lime juice
1 teaspoon grated lime zest
1/3 cup tequila
3 tablespoons Triple Sec
1 (9-inch) baked pie shell

CAMP VERDE TURTLE PECAN PIE

This delectable dessert features one of Arizona's favorite crops. Every February around Valentine's Day, pecan lovers head for Camp Verde's annual pecan festival. This harvest celebration includes pecan judging, a pecan bake-off, pecan wine, and more pecan pies than you can count.

Preheat oven to 350 degrees F. Combine flour and 4 teaspoons of the sugar in a small bowl. Using a fork, stir in butter until mixture forms coarse crumbs. Stir in 1 teaspoon of water. Squeeze the dough into a ball, then press it over the bottom and three-quarters of the way up the sides of a 8-inch springform pan coated with nonstick cooking spray. Bake until pastry is golden brown and firm when pressed, about 20 minutes.

In the meantime, blend the remaining sugar with egg, corn syrup, vanilla, chocolate, and pecans. Pour into warm crust. Return to oven and bake until filling is set when pan is gently shaken, about 30 minutes. Allow to cool at least 30 minutes.

To make caramel sauce, combine 1 tablespoon butter and 5 tablespoons sugar in a saucepan. Cook over high heat until butter is melted and mixture is amber in color. Stir in cream. Pour sauce over cooled pie before serving. *Makes 12 servings*

1/2 cup flour
1/3 cup sugar
3 tablespoons butter, cut into chunks
1 teaspoon water
1 large egg
1/4 cup corn syrup
1 teaspoon vanilla
1/4 cup semisweet chocolate chips
1 to 2 cups pecans, chopped
1 tablespoon butter
5 tablespoons sugar
1/4 cup heavy whipping cream

CHANDLER CHOCOLATE NUT PIE

During the early 1900s, the little farm town of Chandler hosted Fred Astaire, Joan Crawford, Clark Gable, and President Herbert Hoover. These and other luminaries stayed at Chandler's San Marcos Hotel, which boasted the state's first golf course. Chandler is now a bustling suburb, and the San Marcos, with its graceful palm-lined drive, is an oasis of a more elegant age.

Preheat oven to 350 degrees F. Cream together butter and sugar in a large bowl. Add the eggs, corn syrup, salt, and vanilla, mixing well. Stir in chocolate chips, pecans, and bourbon until thoroughly mixed. Pour into pie shell and bake 45 minutes.   *Makes 8 servings*

4 tablespoons butter, softened
1 cup sugar
3 eggs, beaten
3/4 cup light corn syrup
1/4 teaspoon salt
1 teaspoon vanilla
1/2 cup semisweet chocolate chips
3/4 cup pecans, chopped
2 tablespoons bourbon
1 (10-inch) unbaked piecrust

RECIPE NOTES

RECIPE NOTES